ROMANCING YOUR WIFE

DEBRA WHITE SMITH
& DANIEL W. SMITH

HARVEST HOUSE PUBLISHERS

EUGENE, OREGON

Cover by Garborg Design Works, Minneapolis, Minnesota

Every effort has been made to give proper credit for all stories, poems, and quotations. If for any reason proper credit has not been given, please notify the author or publisher and proper notation will be given on future printings.

Published in association with the literary agency of Alive Communications, Inc., 7680 Goddard Street, Suite 200, Colorado Springs, CO 80920

ROMANCING YOUR WIFE

Copyright © 2005 by Debra White Smith and Daniel W. Smith
Published by Harvest House Publishers
Eugene, Oregon 97402
www.harvesthousepublishers.com

Library of Congress Cataloging-in-Publication Data

Smith, Debra White.
   Romancing your wife / Debra White Smith and Daniel W. Smith.
     p. cm.
   Includes bibliographical references.
   ISBN 0-7369-1301-7 (pbk.)
1. Christian men—Religious life. 2. Husbands—Religious life. 3. Marriage—Religious aspects—Christianity. I. Smith, Daniel W., 1960- II. Title
   BV4528.2.S56 2005
   248.8'425—dc22

Printed in the United States of America

05 06 07 08 09 10 11 12 / BP-KB / 10 9 8 7 6 5 4 3 2 1

Contents

Best Friends,
Soul Mates, Lovers

WOULD YOU LIKE TO BE SO ENAMORED with your wife that you can't wait to get home to her? Do you want your wife to be your best friend, your lover, and your sexual playmate? If so, then you desire something many men dream about but never have...something truly special.

Prepare yourself for the unique in this book. The following pages are not a rehash of the same principles you've read in every other marriage book. Instead, we've taken a fresh look at Scripture and developed healthy, balanced concepts. We're offering a new and life-changing approach to your marriage.

As you read this book, realize that you might be required to retrain your thinking patterns, your behavioral norms, and even the way you have viewed Scripture. This might seem painful at first and too big of a risk. But we are confident that the same thing will happen to your marriage that has happened to ours.

After 21 years, we are best friends, soul mates, and lovers. We can't get enough of each other. We are more than mere spouses; we are a blending of two spirits into one. Neither of us is tempted to go outside our marriage for sexual or emotional fulfillment because we are finding an over-abundance of fulfillment with each other.

You may be thinking, "Well, I'm not the only one who needs something new in my approach to marriage. My wife needs help as much as I do!" In that case, we suggest you consult *Romancing Your Husband,* which is a perfect companion to this book. Many husbands buy and read that book before giving it to their wives. As in *Romancing Your Husband,* many chapters in *Romancing Your Wife* apply to both men and women, specifically chapters 2-4, 6, and 8.

Understand that our marriage is a work in progress. Admittedly, we have come through some dark and dysfunctional days together. Many couples may have even divorced over some of the issues we have faced. Much of what you will encounter in this book is the product of two decades of maturity, overcoming our own mistakes, and tenacious labor. As you absorb our words, be aware that you might be challenged by the depth of spiritual growth you will be asked to embrace. Once you start reading the book, don't allow a defeatist attitude of "I'll never measure up" to daunt you. Instead, take one chapter at a time and implement the truths one at a time. Be committed to the turnaround in your marriage. The results will be mind boggling!

In His Service,

Daniel & Debra

Romancing
Your Wife

What My Husband Does Right
by Debra White Smith

- ∾ Daniel always makes me feel needed and appreciated.

- ∾ He never criticizes my body, face, or anything about me.

- ∾ He says he likes me better at a size 12 than a size 8.

- ∾ He delights in any new lingerie purchases and loves me to model them.

- ∾ He's always "chasing" me—continually letting me know he has the hots for me.

- ∾ Any time I make an extra effort to dress up, he goes on and on like I'm Miss America.

- ∾ He doesn't mention my cellulite.

- ∾ He asks me where I want to go when we eat out.

- ∾ He shares his food with me in the restaurant.

- ∾ He is never ashamed to show his emotions to me.

- ∾ He regularly attends church.

1

Treat Her Like a Queen

*And the king loved Esther more than all the women,
and she found favor and kindness with him...
so that he set the royal crown on her
head and made her queen.*

ESTHER 2:17 NASB

My son, Brett, is an incredible little boy. At the ripe old age of nine, he has developed a pattern of treating me like a queen. Sometimes when we're sitting beside each other, he puts his arm around my shoulders. At night, if I lie down beside him, he occasionally wants me to lie on his arm. He then pats my shoulder. Any time we're alone in our family van, we hold hands from one seat to the other.

The other day it was raining, and he met me at the door with an umbrella. From there, he walked me to the van, making sure my head was shielded from the rain. He didn't care whether or not he got wet, just as long as I was dry. He even hurried forward to open the van door for me.

Any time he perceives I'm hurting, whether it's a stubbed toe or an emotional ache, he's right there beside me saying, "Mama, are you okay? Is there anything I can do for you?"

The other day, we went fishing. After our family of four had been there awhile, none of us had had much luck. Brett decided that the best fishing spot was farther up the pier. So he got a lawn chair and plopped it down. Instead of claiming the spot for his own, he said, "Mama, you need to come sit here and fish. I think this is a good spot. You'll catch something here!" With that declaration, he threw my line in just the "right spot." With a smile, I agreed to his suggestion, accepted the rod and reel, and claimed the chair.

When I arrive home from the grocery store, my son hurries outside and says, "Mama, do you need some help? Here, let me take that heavy bag. You don't need to carry that."

Recently we were at a wedding reception. I offered to get my husband a bowl of gumbo when I got mine. He was thankful for the offer. When I got to the buffet line, my son was right beside me. "I came to carry Dad's bowl," he said with an assuring smile. "I don't want you to have to carry both bowls."

After we settled back at our table, I looked across at my aunt and beamed. "Brett is starting to treat me just like Daniel does— like I'm a queen."

"I've given up on any man ever treating me that way," she admitted.

> *If a man has enough "horse sense" to*
> *treat his wife like a thoroughbred,*
> *she will never be an old nag.*
>
> —ANONYMOUS

Our Story

Daniel and I have known about each other our whole lives. Our parents were great friends when we were tiny. My family moved away from Daniel's hometown before I was in elementary school. My whole childhood, I remember my parents mentioning Daniel's family. My grandmother often spoke highly of them, as well, since they all went to the same church.

We moved back to our hometown when I was 15. I'll never forget that first Sunday when I walked into the small church and saw Daniel sitting on the pew. Even then, I enjoyed what I saw. He was 19 and an "older man." I liked his football-player physique and his soft-spoken manners that contradicted the "man's man" exterior. Before the week was out, we were meeting at church and social gatherings, and I was shamelessly flirting with Daniel.

Both our parents saw some sparks flying, and they were glad. At first, Daniel told his mother he thought I was too young. Admittedly, four years difference is a significant number of years when the girl is just 15. However, my father was so impressed with Daniel and his family that he okayed my going out with him.

The next few years were some of the hardest of my life. Due to tragic circumstances, my family fell apart. My parents divorced. I lived with my father and soon found myself responsible for much of my personal maintenance. In other words, if I wanted my clothes washed, I did the laundry. If I wanted a meal, I cooked it. If I wanted a car, I worked, saved money, and bought the vehicle.

The whole time Daniel and I dated, he doted on me like I was the only woman in the world. He would often come over and we'd do some really "romantic" things like hanging out laundry to dry (we didn't have a dryer) or cooking a meal. He even went with my father and inspected my first car for me—to make sure the vehicle was safe and worth the $800 I had saved to pay for it.

Looking back, I see that along with God, Daniel was my backbone during those difficult years. I was able to cling to him, my pillar of strength, and he helped me survive.

I would love to tell you that Daniel never hurt me, and I never broke his heart. But I can't. Looking back now, Daniel and I both realize that we were emotional cripples. And while we deeply cared for each other, over the years we each wounded the other as well.

We got married when I had just turned 19 and he was about to turn 23. Neither of us came from moneyed families, but Daniel had worked hard to pay for an engagement ring big enough to strangle a gorilla. The day he slipped the wedding band on my finger, I became my husband's cherished queen. Once, he spent his whole Christmas bonus on a china curio just for me. There was no task too difficult or demeaning for him to do for me. Early in our marriage I accidentally flushed my bracelet down the toilet. He and our neighbor fished through our septic tank until they found the bracelet. Just as Daniel did before we were married, he continued to stand by my side and offered a strong arm in whatever task I pursued.

Even though we both still struggled with emotional baggage and each grappled with how to have a healthy marriage, personal support was Daniel's strong suit. He never wavered when I decided to get serious about college. I was 24 then, and we'd been married five years. When my college career was young, I worked full-time just as Daniel did. He attended my junior college graduation and then my graduation for my bachelor's degree. He beamed the whole time and quietly told me how proud he was of me.

However, I stopped working part of the way through graduate school and gave birth to our son. Soon, I became queen for two males in the household. My husband continued to work and supported me as I finished a master's degree in English. He attended graduation with me and held our son as I sat through the ceremony and walked across the stage to accept my diploma. I was 33.

During my mid-twenties, I had begun to write and hoped to develop a career in book publishing. Daniel did nothing to stop my dreams. He attended writer's conferences with me, listened to me chatter on about the market, and admired my written words. For eight years, he watched as I pounded the doors of the writing industry and gained little ground. Even though he did make some mistakes in our marriage—as did I—never once did he tell me I should toss aside my dreams or that he was tired of my spending so much money on submitting manuscripts and networking at conferences. Instead, he applauded my tiny successes and encouraged me toward doing more.

Finally, in 1997 I began to sell a significant number of books to a variety of publishers. My husband cheered all the louder!

Soon, we adopted a little girl from Vietnam. So, we now had two children, ages two and four. Daniel shouldered the parenting burden with me. We *both* sacrificed together for our children. Because I was and still am radically committed to my family, there were times when Saturday was the only day I had to write. Armed with a diaper bag and a stroller, Daniel would take the kids to the zoo, which would give me almost all day to produce my manuscripts.

Still, he quietly worked the same job he had held for over 15 years.

Eventually, "Debra's writing career" turned into a "Daniel and Debra" ministry. He began to share a significant responsibility in my speaking engagements—including offering his musical talents and singing special music. One day, we began to talk about the possibility of his resigning his job and joining me full-time as ministry manager.

During one of these talks Daniel shared his lifelong dream with me. He had wanted to own his own business since he was a kid. I had been married to him for about 17 years at this point and never knew of his desire. Never once had he said, "Move over with you and your goals. It's *my* turn!" Instead, he had selflessly empowered me to pursue my hopes while putting his deepest desires on hold.

The selflessness of his love struck me full force. I saw in his eyes unbridled admiration. And I told him that I would do everything in my power to enable him to pursue his own business...even if that meant giving up everything I'd accomplished. Instead, he insisted we work together to enable his dream.

Daniel is the mechanical genius sort, and he has a strong need for that gift to be released. He received information about a locksmith training school and enrolled. I applauded him and told him I believed in him. After Daniel finished the training, he was able to establish his own home-based business. As with any new business, it struggled to survive. But I wouldn't let him fall into thinking he should end his venture. Instead, I encouraged him to stay true to his vision.

By this point, I was *determined* that Daniel should succeed in his lifelong aspirations no matter what. So, I became his assistant, doing whatever I could to help him. Before he quit his other job, I answered his phone and identified myself as "the locksmith's secretary." I took messages, forwarded calls, and spoke with customers.

Eventually, my writing and speaking income increased to the point that Daniel was able to quit his other job and embrace his dream of being his own boss. He also stepped into the role of manager for our Real Life Ministries. Now, we work together every day and call each other "boss." I'm his secretary on call, and he's my manager. We are each filling a supportive role in the other's life and loving every minute of it!

I have gradually come to realize that there are some men who would have never empowered their wives as my husband has empowered me. They may have never viewed their wives as royalty. Some may even go to their graves and never understand that to truly cherish a woman they must die to every scrap of self-interest.

But Daniel understands this...and much more. He recognized a gift within me and wanted to see it mature. He set aside his own desires—never even mentioning them—in order to see me succeed. This level of selfless devotion is a rare find—even with Christian men. Ironically, if my husband had demanded that I not pursue an education and my writing, he very likely would still not know the fulfillment of his own dream due to financial obligations. Daniel's very selflessness lead to the achievement of his own goals.

Even though our marriage was far from perfect, Daniel had mastered a key component for creating a marriage that would last. Because he was so supportive and lifted his spouse (me!) up, I in turn could give my all to him.

As the Father has loved me, so have I loved you.
Now remain in my love. If you obey my commands,
you will remain in my love, just as I have obeyed my
Father's commands and remain in his love. I have told you this
so that my joy may be in you and that your joy may be complete.
My command is this: Love each other as I have loved you.
Greater love has no one than this, that he lay
down his life for his friends.

JOHN 15:9-13

The Royal Code of Honor

At this point, you may already be feeling a bit challenged. In many ways you probably already sacrifice for your wife, such as providing support and a place to live. But maybe the little, daily things slip by. Perhaps you're even at a loss of exactly where to start in treating your wife like a queen. After all, there are no college courses titled "Queen Bee 101." And frankly, there may be few fathers who bestow their wives with the adoration and respect that my husband lavishes upon me in front of our son. So, chances are high you didn't see selfless love actively modeled.

If you *are* grappling for the elements of treating your wife like a queen, the renowned story of Esther in the Old Testament offers a classic example of some basic concepts that will take your marriage to a new dimension. According to the book of Esther, King Xerxes was enamored with Esther from their first acquaintance. From there, he wasted no time ranking her as queen and making certain she understood her position.

Customs and cultures have drastically changed since this story occurred, and there are some elements from the story of Esther we *should not* apply to marriages today. Admittedly, there is nothing holy about the way Xerxes treated his first queen, Vashti. In a drunken fit of revelry, he viewed her as a sex object to be paraded in front of his intoxicated friends. He and his buddies had been drinking alcohol for a week! When Vashti refused such humiliation, he divorced her.

Next, Xerxes approached the process of choosing a new queen like our modern process of buying an automobile. He "test drove" numerous virginal girls one at a time. In other words, he kept sleeping with innocent young women in search of the "perfect queen." Then, when he didn't care to make the latest innocent his queen, he placed her in his harem for later use and prepared for another "test drive" (see Esther 1–2). In their book *Two Become One: God's Blueprint for Couples*, Donald and Robbie Joy wisely point out that traditionally, components of the story of Esther have been misapplied: The drunken Xerxes has been venerated while Vashti has been labeled as a rebellious wife.[1] Bible scholar Adam Clarke, states, "What woman, possessing even a common share of prudence and modesty, could consent to expose herself to the view of such a group of drunken Bacchanalians?"[2] Obviously, some of Xerxes' actions don't fall under the category of a good Christian model for marriages or the God-approved behavior of a husband.

Nevertheless, once Xerxes chose Esther as queen, Scripture details that he treated her like royalty. Despite the fact that Xerxes did do some things wrong, men today can still glean insight from some of Xerxes' actions toward his new queen. As you read the following observations from the book of Esther, imagine how these suggestions might impact your marriage.

> ✍ *Xerxes honored Esther.* "So [Xerxes] set a royal crown on her head and made her queen....And the king gave a great banquet, Esther's banquet, for all his nobles and officials. He proclaimed a holiday throughout the provinces and distributed gifts with royal liberality" (Esther 2:17-18).
>
> If you want to make your wife feel like a queen, declare an annual, biannual, or quarterly holiday at your house.

Name the day after her. On that day, prepare (or buy) a banquet just for your wife, and name the banquet after her. Set her at the table with great pomp and don't allow her to assist in any aspect of the meal—including cleanup. Buy her a gift she will find special. If you're on a budget, you can still purchase flowers from a department or grocery store. Repeat the banquet every year, twice a year, or every three months, according to what fits your schedule and budget.

∾ *Xerxes listened to Esther.* "On the third day Esther put on her royal robes and stood in the inner court of the palace, in front of the king's hall. The king was sitting on his royal throne in the hall, facing the entrance. When he saw Queen Esther standing in the court, he was pleased with her and held out to her the gold scepter that was in his hand. So Esther approached and touched the tip of the scepter" (Esther 5:1-2).

While normal guys don't sit around on a royal throne and hold scepters, sometimes wives can feel as if a man's "kingdom" is more important to him than she is. A modern man's "kingdom" can take the shape of his car, motorcycle, sports, career, ministry, or civic clubs.

According to the ancient laws, Xerxes could have had Esther killed for approaching him without prior permission. Likewise, a wife may feel that asking for her husband's time is risking emotional death. If the husband responds abruptly, impatiently, or shows no interest, she will feel as if she has been emotionally stabbed.

If you really want your wife to feel like royalty, then listen to her. Be still. Look her in the eyes. And revere every word she says.

∞ *Xerxes offered Esther equal share in his kingdom.* "Then the king asked, 'What is it, Queen Esther? What is your request? Even up to half the kingdom, it will be given you'" (Esther 5:3). Amazingly, Xerxes made this same offer to Esther three times (see 5:6 and 7:2).

Recently, my husband began receiving some inheritance money after his mother's death. We put most of the money in a savings account. The other day, I was talking to Daniel and referred to the money as "your money." My husband looked at me with a determined fierceness in his eyes and said, "No. That money is *our* money."

What is your attitude toward the money you earn and all you own? Do you view your possessions as just yours? Or do you honor your wife enough to view your income and possessions as hers, too? If you do, then you will ask for and respect her thoughts in every financial decision and purchase you make—even if she never generates an income outside the home.

This mind-set transcends material possessions. Wives are most esteemed when their husbands pour out their talents, strengths, abilities, insight, and wisdom in honor of them because these qualities are the very essence of who he is. This works the same when wives pour out their gifts and abilities for their husbands.

∞ *Xerxes defended Esther's honor.* "Just as the king returned from the palace garden to the banquet hall, Haman was falling on the couch where Esther was reclining. The king exclaimed, 'Will he even molest the queen while she is with me in the house?'...The king said, 'Hang him on [the gallows]!'" (Esther 7:8-9).

Xerxes's example underscores a vital truth: A husband who truly regards his wife as his queen won't allow another person to demean her, disrespect her, or harm her in any way. Such a husband will not permit his children to exhibit any impertenance toward his wife or allow members of his family of origin to smear her reputation or assault her name to him. This husband won't participate in any conversation or action that puts his wife down. He won't adopt marital concepts that demote his wife in any way. Furthermore, when a husband with royal intent is with his wife, his words, expressions, and gestures will reflect the adoration he feels for her.

Romancing
by Ray N. Hawkins

I prayed,
cried,
sighed.
I schemed
screamed
dreamed.
I searched,
lurched
perched,
precariously
in many
strange places
for ways
to romance
my wife.

I was,
mysterious,
adventurous
spontaneous.
Without success.
Romance
faded.
I became
jaded.
Until
I gave up
trying
and began
being.

Romancing
is more than
dancing,
soft lights,
gifts,
helpful
though
they be.

Romancing
is togetherness.
Heart sharing,
mind enriching,
spirit uplifting.
Talking,
touching,
laughing,
playing
create
romance's
atmosphere
where love
thrives
as lovers
breathe.[3]

From Daniel

You've probably already guessed that I'm not a high-powered CEO sort. I'm not a jet-setter type by any means. I'm an ordinary guy who screams during the Super Bowl, would give my right arm for a hole in one, and enjoys singing and playing instruments. I'm also a mechanical buff.

But there's nothing ordinary about the way I feel about my wife. I'm *nuts* about her! I'd do anything in the world for her. *Anything!* There are some days I find myself falling all over both her and me just to serve her.

I have to be honest, though, and admit that I have had my share of issues. There have been times when, due to my past, I didn't really know how to show Debra the depth of my love. But even in my darkest days I still tried be thoughtful and supportive.

Through the years, I've watched men who ignore their wives and have no clue what the word "cherish" means. Furthermore, if I were to suggest they should treat their wives like queens, they'd probably say something brilliant like "Huh?" For instance, a wife might be juggling a baby car seat, a bag of groceries, and a squirming toddler while her husband is too busy talking with a friend or watching TV to help her. When I see situations like this, I get so exasperated I usually wind up offering assistance myself. Frankly, there have been times when I was tempted to shoot glares at inconsiderate husbands.

Occasionally, I've even noticed some of these women seem to have a hopeless hunger gnawing at their souls. They silently say, "Will my husband ever cherish me as much as this man cherishes his wife?" Sad as it may seem, I've learned to be careful in some of these situations. I'm afraid my honest desire to simply be helpful and understanding may be misconstrued. But frankly, if I were as desperate to be appreciated as some of the neglected wives I've noticed, I might misconstrue a motive or two myself.

Since I often see some women married to thoughtless husbands, I cringe to think that I'd ever become a thoughtless husband myself. Therefore, my life's goal now is to do everything in my power to make Debra feel like my queen. I want to empower her to be all she can be and to help her on the way. If that means carrying in the groceries, I will do it. If that means managing the kids while she writes, I will do it. If that means carrying her purse all over the United States because she's just had surgery and the thing weighs a ton, I will do it. (I think she must put chunks of steel in that purse!)

I have committed my life to making my wife feel like pampered royalty. As a man of honor, I will offer nothing less.

Prayer Points for Romance

- Pray that God will begin showing you specific ways you can make your wife feel like royalty.

- Ask the Lord to reveal any wrong attitudes you may harbor toward your wife.

- Pray that God will begin to stir you about any erroneous concepts you have embraced that make you feel superior to your wife in any way.

- Beseech the Lord to give you a new vision of what your marriage can be like if you dare to implement the truths from this chapter.

- Pray that God will impart to you a new realization and understanding of selfless love.

Romantic Notions

Arise, come, my darling; my
beautiful one, come with me.

SONG OF SONGS 2:13

What I Did

Debra and I were attending a Boy Scout function with our son, Brett. I was required to be there early with Brett, and my wife was arriving about an hour later. It started raining, and I became concerned over whether or not Debra had an umbrella. (With two young kids, our umbrella collection stays scattered.) I went out to my van and found an umbrella. Then I called Debra. She was on her way. I asked her if she had an umbrella. She said no, so, I told her I'd meet her at her van and walk her into the building.

My Reason

I'm wild about my wife and want to spend my life making her feel indulged and adored.

How I Felt

I was warmed that she was thrilled with my effort. Also, extending this kindness to her made me feel needed. Honestly, I was a little glad that she didn't have the umbrella so I could be of help.

The Obstacles I Overcame

My main concern involved timing. Since I was participating in the Boy Scout event, I didn't want to get so distracted that I forgot to meet her outside. That would have been a disaster after telling her I'd be there.

My Wife's Response

Debra was *so* appreciative and impressed that I had thought of something so seemingly small. She hugged me and beamed and told me she was spoiled rotten! The way she laughed, I think she enjoys my spoiling her.

What I Wish I Had Done

I don't have any regrets on this one.

Budget Suggestions

This idea cost me time and the effort of caring enough to act. Sometimes I think it's easier to throw some money-based idea at our wives for a special occasion than it is to be considerate and thoughtful every day of the week.

Special Note

If you'd like to explore more thoughtful and innovative ways to romance your wife, check out chapter 7 for more endearing encounter ideas!

What My Husband Does Right

by Jennifer Hale

~ My husband is an epileptic. Despite the fact that we cannot get his condition under control right now, he is still the best man in the world to me. God blessed me good! He does not let his seizure disorder stop him from being the best husband and father that he is able to be.

~ My husband takes me away for special weekends.

~ He took me on a shopping spree to Victoria's Secret that ended up being his own private fashion show.

~ For my twenty-fifth birthday my husband bought me my first horse. We went to an auction, had dinner at Red Lobster, and then went shopping. Since we own a quarter horse business this was a big deal to me.

~ We made out on a very secluded road in the county in which we live.

~ He brings me flowers. And over the past nine years, I have rarely been without them. I hope this one never ends.

~ He sends me a note or card at least once a week.[1]

2

Becoming One

*For this reason a man will leave his father and mother
and be united to his wife, and the two will become one flesh.
This is a profound mystery.*
EPHESIANS 5:31

BUSINESSMEN HAVE IT SO GOOD! Somebody with a lot of insight invented a great purse for men and called it a briefcase. I've wanted a purse like that for years—with all the pockets and slots and holders. That way everything has its place, and there's no chance of the mass confusion so many women's purses lend themselves to. But they don't make a briefcase in the size I need. Most briefcases are proportionately created to fit a hulking man, not an average-sized woman. For years I've looked for a case that is about half the size of a normal briefcase but a little thicker. I had almost despaired of ever finding what I needed until a recent trip to the office supply store.

There, nestled on the shelf, I found it! A case exactly the size I had been searching for. To top it off, someone had designed it in silver, so it looked less like a traditional briefcase. I was elated! I bought my new "purse," took it home, and showed it to my best friend—my husband.

Daniel said, "Oh! That's so pretty! But I don't think you'll be able to get all your stuff in that case. It looks kind of small."

"But you don't know who you're dealing with!" I said, "I can make this work. I really can! It's *exactly* what I've been looking for!"

Daniel shook his head and smirked (of all the nerve!) as I flopped open my new "purse" on the dining room table and began to fill it with my stuff. He followed that smirk with a chuckle and leaned against the breakfast bar.

"I really think that's a great case," he said with an indulgent smile, "and I could even use it in my locksmith business." Daniel crossed his arms. "I've got some papers I've been needing a case just like that for."

I did something really spiritual—like narrowing my eyes and said, "Not on your life, Buddy! You aren't going to get my purse!"

He laughed outright. "Yes, I will," he claimed. "There's no way you're going to fit all the junk from your purse in there. And when you accept defeat, I'll be glad to accept the case."

By this time, I was more determined than ever to make the "purse" work. I was in the throes of arranging and rearranging all my electronics and other important stuff (that my best friend had the audacity to call junk). After a particularly exasperating round of fighting to shut the case against the bulge within, I looked back at Daniel and declared with a teasing grin, "I'm not going to give you this case. If I can't get it to work, I'm taking it back to the office store. If you want it, you'll have to go buy it yourself!"

"Oooo," he taunted, "you're a *mean*-spirited woman!"

We both enjoyed an abundance of laughter.

"Just wait," I vowed, "I will make this case work. It's exactly… what…I…need," I finished through gritted teeth as I attempted to close the thing once more.

By the next morning, I realized my dreams of the silver case becoming my new purse would not be fulfilled. With the defeat of a gracious warrior, I removed my possessions from the case and extended it to my husband. "Here," I said, "you were right. I hope you enjoy my new purse."

Daniel chuckled and took my "purse" without so much as an apology or a sympathetic pat on the back. The last time I saw my "purse" it was in his locksmith van, full of *his* stuff. I promise, the briefcase stuck its tongue out at me and said, "Naaa, na-na-na-na!" like a spoiled child!

I thought, *My husband took my purse! What's next? My panty-hose?*

> *Whoso findeth a wife findeth a good thing,*
> *and obtaineth favour of the* LORD....
> *A man that hath friends must shew himself friendly;*
> *and there is a friend that sticketh closer than a brother.*
> PROVERBS 18:22,24 KJV

"One-Couples"

One of the primary characteristics of a couple who has become one is that there is an unrestrained freedom in their relationship. They enjoy being together so much that other people delight in being with them just to soak up the joy. "One-couples" get along so well that everyday activities, such as buying a briefcase, are turned into a celebration of their bliss with a cheerful round of banter. Serious arguments are rare because one-couples are so busy having the same thoughts that they seldom disagree. Due to this unity of mind and spirit, they often finish each other's sentences.

One-couples frequently do things like come home at the end of the day with a grocery bag full of similar items. "I thought we'd have Frito pie for dinner," the wife says as she pulls out a jumbo bag of Fritos. "No way!" the husband exclaims. "Look!" he says as he holds up the bag of Fritos and can of chili he just bought.

When the two have become one, they are usually known for the way they tease each other and flirt like teenagers. Or, if their personalities don't lend themselves to this behavior, they enjoy a goofy grin when they see each other. If they have young kids, the children sense the harmony and freedom and say things like, "You two are love birds." A child of one-couple parents might draw a heart on a steamed-up bathroom mirror and write "Mom and Dad" in the middle. (Our children do this sort of stuff all the time.)

One-couples are often easy to spot. You'll find them in the crowd laughing at the same stupid joke nobody else got. They're usually the ones wrapped up together in a blanket near the bonfire while all the other "old married couples" have congregated into same-sex circles to complain about each other. Or they might cancel plans with friends just to be together because they can't get enough of each other.

Most husbands and wives start their marriages with the idea that they are going to be one-couples. But once the reality of personal imperfections and negative behavior patterns appear, many decide the whole one-couple idea is just a fantasy that doesn't exist for anyone. Well, Daniel and I can testify that being a one-couple isn't a mere fantasy. After years of hard work, it has become our reality—and it can be yours as well!

As you read the following foundation for becoming a one-couple, understand that we have not always been this type of couple. The first decade of our marriage was fraught with so many negative issues, we're sure couples in similar marriages may have divorced. Fifteen years ago, our whole conversation regarding the purse-case would have gone something like...

> "What's the silver thing?"
> "It's just a case I bought. I hope I can make it into a purse."
> "Oh, okay. I'm heading to the golf course."
> "Okay. I'll be doing some reading."
> Exchange a respectful kiss.
> "Goodbye."

Understand that becoming one will mean both husband and wife must set aside the self and any destructive behaviors in preference for the spouse. (See chapter 3.) According to Donald and

Robbie Joy, "Self-centered human beings persistently drift toward arrogance and exclusion, but faith requires us to dance the dance of respect and unity."[2] Jesus Christ said, "Whoever finds his life will lose it, and whoever loses his life for my sake will find it" (Matthew 10:39). One-couples have learned to radically live out these words from Christ. As a result, they have found a unity of spirit that defies explanation.

There are many traits of one-couples, which will be touched upon throughout this book, but one significant mind-set is proven to be the cornerstone for this rare marital experience. As you continue forth, understand that the pathway to oneness is a journey. Don't expect this marital existence to descend upon you after one week. The process may take several months or several years, depending on where you are starting in your marriage. Also, understand that implementing *all* of chapter 3 is a necessity to becoming a one-couple. But once you do begin to see the fruit of your efforts, be prepared for the mysterious to unfold and for your marriage to undergo a metamorphosis.

> *When a man marries a woman, they become one,*
> *but the trouble starts when they try to decide which one.*
>
> ANONYMOUS

Free to Be

The foundation for becoming a one-couple is to allow your spouse the freedom to be herself. One-couples permit each other to exhibit individual strengths and weaknesses and to accept each other exactly the way they are. Too many times I encounter people who have read a book or gone to a conference and come away with a cookie-cutter stereotype for what they believe they and their spouses are supposed to be. Often, Scripture is even "strip-mined"—emphasizing some Scriptures and ignoring others—to provide a narrow, definitive role of what a husband and a wife should be. (See chapter 6.) From there, even spiritual gifts are sometimes assigned based on gender.

But determining roles, gifts, and tasks based strictly on gender seldom—if ever—is fulfilling for both husband and wife. God made each of us to be unique individuals that often complement our spouses. Frankly, Daniel and I have never conformed to the molds many well-meaning people say we're "supposed" to fill.

- ∽ *We don't fit spiritually.* Daniel is very intuitive spiritually. He has a major gift of discernment, along with a gift of helping others. I'm a prayer warrior and serious student of the Bible who also writes nonfiction and fiction books. I have the gift of speaking and have had the honor of addressing thousands of men and women nationwide.

- ∽ *We don't fit the molds emotionally.* Daniel is not overtly assertive, except when it comes to sex, mechanics, sports, and eating. He also is neither unfeeling nor unable to express his emotions. He is soft-spoken, low-key, greatly nurturing, and sensitive. Daniel is as intuitive emotionally as he is spiritually. I've never been moody for any reason. I'm not dependent, fickle, or different every day. I am assertive, intense, high-energy, outspoken, outgoing, and goal-oriented.

- ∽ *Finally, we don't fit the stereotypes mentally.* I'm analytical and decisive, and I adjust well to change. As a matter of fact, I *love* change—especially if it appears to offer improvement. While Daniel is also analytical, he needs time to process decisions. He really does not like change. We both are highly competitive when it comes to sports.

None of this is good or bad. It's just the way we are. But it's not the way some people insist we should be according to their biblical interpretation. In order to fit the traditional molds advocated by some, Daniel and I would both have to undergo personality transplants. We would have to change the very essence of who we are. That would mean altering the things that attracted us to each other in the first place. Unfortunately, that is exactly what some misguided couples spend their entire lives trying to do. Instead of honoring their individual strengths and gifts, they try to fit arbitrary, assigned roles. Because of this, they go to their graves as a two-couple and never experience the bliss of truly being one.

> *For by the grace given me I say to every one of you:*
> *Do not think of yourself more highly than you ought,*
> *but rather think of yourself with sober judgment,*
> *in accordance with the measure of faith God has given you.*
> *Just as each of us has one body with many members,*
> *and these members do not all have the same function,*
> *so in Christ we who are many form one body, and each member*
> *belongs to all the others. We have different gifts,*
> *according to the grace given us.*
>
> ROMANS 12:3-6

I don't know many couples who fit the cookie-cutter roles that insist every man holds one set of spiritual, emotional, and mental strengths and every woman holds another. An enormous amount of freedom descended upon our union when I decided to let Daniel be who he really is and stopped trying to hoist him into a role that simply did not fit his personality or areas of giftedness. When that bondage slipped away, we were spiritually liberated to blend our unique set of spiritual gifts into a whole and impact our family and home as one.

> *While strict definitions of married roles might fit the*
> *personality and gifts of the person who developed them*

*and a few people with identical makeups, everybody else
is left to believe his or her spouse is inadequate.*

Debra White Smith

If in your mind you are thinking something like "All women are _____," and your wife doesn't fit that, then you'll spend your entire marriage disenchanted. Maybe she's like me and has strengths she's "not supposed" to have as a Christian woman. You might have even been taught "all women are _____." Then, you spend your whole life thinking your wife isn't in line with the Word of God. Or maybe you've believed that her weakest areas are supposed to be her strengths. If so, you may be blinded to the beauty of the strengths she does have. Next thing you know, you'll be looking at somebody else's wife and thinking, "Now *she* is _____." And you'll become more and more disillusioned with your marriage. Soon, you'll be unable to see the unique set of strengths the Lord has placed in your wife. A man in that frame of mind cannot cherish his wife. Instead, he'll be tempted to cherish that other woman.

It's all too common for people to use the Bible to support blind prejudices, limiting customs, and thoughtless assumptions, while ignoring significant scriptures that refute the theories. This brings bondage and legalism into marriage. Bondage and legalism create a splintering effect upon the union. Instead of the husband and wife working together as a unit in all things and being free to express their individual strengths, they are trapped into molds that don't fit either of them. Like bad-fitting shoes, these molds will eventually rub calluses on the marriage and warp the partners into distorted behaviors that stop them from being who they really are. Instead of embracing their marital existence with freedom and zest, the husband and wife are forced to perform like masked attendees at a masquerade party. According to Robert M. Hicks, "Some Christian couples begin to view their marriage as a giant commercial for God. In public, they play as if they are happy and fulfilled in order to show outsiders how good God is. In reality, their family life and marriage may be a sham."[3]

For instance, I once listened to a speaker who explained how his wife didn't have the gift of managing a checking account and paying bills. He kept getting past due statements because his wife just couldn't keep up with the whole financial process. Finally, when he asked her about the financial mess, she started crying. He said that he soon realized he was expecting his wife to do something no woman was ever equipped to do. The man concluded, "God did not create women to handle pressure."

What this man did was use his wife's individual set of weaknesses as a mold for what every other woman was supposed to be. His very thought process also blinded him to his wife's strengths. Ironically, the same woman he claimed couldn't handle pressure also homeschooled her children. From experience I can guarantee that homeschooling is a pressure-filled endeavor!

In our union, Daniel is the one who can't stand juggling the checking accounts. Through the years, we've tried letting him manage the money. While I've never seen him cry over the job, I have seen him on the verge of pulling out his hair. The whole process drives him crazy! He *does* take care of his business account, but the rest is up to me. Why? Because that is *my* strength. It is not his. If God had given either a husband or wife all strengths, we wouldn't need each other. I could get really disillusioned really fast if I suddenly decided Daniel should exhibit all of my spiritual, emotional, and mental strengths along with all of his and manifest them in our home. That's not even logical. Nevertheless, many times key scriptures have been isolated to prove this error. Husbands and wives are both encouraged to think in these limiting terms. From there, the wife develops a huge case of disenchantment with her husband because he "falls short" of being everything without her. What so many men don't seem to understand is that disenchanted women don't seduce their husbands (see chapter 6).

Recently, I encountered someone saying that women were better at cooking than men. My first thought was, "Oh, so that's the reason why *Emeril Live,* the TV show featuring the acclaimed Italian chef, is such a flop! And why there has never been a male chef since the beginning of creation!" If I were to accept such rigid, stereotypical thinking, I would have been exceedingly offended when my mechanical-genius husband declared that he was going to learn to cook. I could have gone into a "real men don't cook" mental tailspin and looked down on him for his honest interest. I would have also missed out on his Sara Lee Cheesecake that's so good it makes me howl!

Likewise, if Daniel had been determined to force me into someone else's preset mold, he would have been threatened by my ability to juggle three checking accounts, a savings account, and handle all our family investments.

Then we both could have lived the rest of our lives thinking our spouse just doesn't measure up. When spouses embrace this mind-set, they block the opportunity to become one. Instead, they stay two. When a couple is two, they don't typically meet each other's needs. They fall into believing things like "no man can meet his wife's emotional needs, so the wife should turn to same-sex friends to have her needs for intimacy fulfilled" or "no wife ever completely satisfies her husband's sexual desires, so the husband is destined to live one breath away from committing sexual sins for the rest of his life." Such two-couples live their whole lives in a state of perpetual disappointment.

Furthermore, the disappointment is wrapped in fear. Legalism breeds fear. That's how Satan keeps people in bondage. He creates a rule-based mentality and scares people into believing if they don't keep "this rigid set of guidelines" that have nothing to do with morality, then God will be angry.

One-Couples...

- ∽ think in terms of "we and us," not "me and you" or "my and me."

- ∽ are free to be themselves and exercise all their gifts.

- ∽ have marriages that are love-based, not rule- or control-based.

- ∽ don't care which spouse earns the most. Love and respect thrive based on the essence of who the spouse is, not what the spouse earns.

- ∽ do everything possible to empower each other. One spouse never looks at the other and says, "Your role is to empower me." Or "You're supposed to pour yourself into *me* while I pursue *my* interests."

- ∽ aren't threatened by each other's gifts and talents, but freely applaud each other's accomplishments.

- ∽ are best friends.

- ∽ argue infrequently, because they are of one mind.

- ∽ live by Jesus Christ's Golden Rule: "So *in everything*, do to others what you would have them do to you" (Matthew 7:12, emphasis added). This includes *everything*, just as Jesus said—even the marriage concepts you embrace.

- ∽ don't believe one of them is spiritually superior to the other or has a deeper spiritual knowledge on all subjects at all times.

- ∽ have their needs met and enjoy a thriving relationship— emotionally and sexually.

- ∽ don't look to each other as a replacement for a relationship with God.

- ∽ make decisions by consensus, not by powerplays.

Take it from a couple who has broken free of the legalistic concepts, God will *not* be angry. Instead, He will give you each the courage to admit that you can learn from each other on all levels. Daniel has had life experiences I have not had. He's had spiritual struggles I have not had. He has spiritual gifts I do not have. Therefore, I can learn from his experiences, his gifts, and the strengths he has gleaned. Likewise, I have had spiritual struggles and life experiences Daniel has not had. I have spiritual gifts Daniel does not have. Therefore, he is wise enough to accept that he can also learn from my gifts, strengths, and experiences as well.

Another example includes our ministry endeavors. Daniel has more extensive musical training than I do. So when he corrects my singing, I adjust to what he says and ask few questions. This is his strength. Likewise, the writing of this book reflects an area of my ministry strength. I have a degree in English he does not have. Daniel would be crazy to decide that God's will is for him to step in and take charge of this book project because it's a ministry endeavor—and his role is to oversee all ministry activities.

Spiritually, neither of us believes that one of us has all the answers in all situations or that God does or will communicate with one of us more than the other. Because of this attitude of mutual submission and mutual respect and a spiritual partnership, God has showered our marriage with so much freedom and joy it splashes onto our children and everybody we encounter. Neither of us is disillusioned with the other in any way or expecting the other to be something we cannot be or will *never* be!

We share everything—including praying with our children and teaching them the Word of God *together*. Furthermore, we give each other spiritual support. We pray together, read the Bible together, and each show an interest in the other's spiritual welfare. One of us doesn't expect the other to suddenly turn into a spiritual super-giant that has most, if not all, the answers and all spiritual skills. Instead, we're who we are before God and with

each other. And together, we're allowing the Holy Spirit to impact
our home through each of our unique sets of gifts.

> *So God created man in his own image, in the image of God*
> *he created him; male and female he created them.*
> *God blessed them and said to them,*
> *"Be fruitful and increase in number;*
> *fill the earth and subdue it.*
> *Rule [together] over the fish of the sea and the birds*
> *of the air and over every living creature that*
> *moves on the ground."*
>
> GENESIS 1:27-28

> *In the Lord, however, woman is not independent of man,*
> *nor is man independent of woman.*
>
> 1 CORINTHIANS 11:11

> *There is neither Jew nor Greek, slave nor free,*
> *male nor female, for you are all one in Christ Jesus.*
>
> GALATIANS 3:28

If you dare to allow the Lord to transform your marital mind-
set, His Spirit will be unleashed to fully engulf your union and
make you and your spouse, not only one, but also best friends.
You see, a wonderful friendship naturally unfolds between a husband and wife who are allowed to be who they really are and who
allow each other to exhibit their strengths. A husband and wife
who view each other as best friends will *want* to do things together
and please each other. One of the greatest compliments my husband gave me happened the day I was offering to arrange a golfing
trip for him and one of his male friends. He said, "I don't want to
go with any of them. I want to go with *you!*"

What unique spiritual, mental, and emotional strengths does
your wife have? Are you willing to allow her these strengths even

if they don't fit the stereotype? What unique weaknesses does she have? Are you willing to use your strengths to empower her weak areas? Furthermore, are you willing to admit that you, too, have weak areas—spiritually, emotionally, and mentally—and then allow her to use her strengths to empower your weaknesses? If you and she both will agree to this new, freeing mentality, you will have overcome one of the major barriers to truly becoming one.

> *If you have any encouragement from being united with Christ,*
> *if any comfort from his love, if any fellowship with the Spirit,*
> *if any tenderness and compassion, then make my joy complete*
> *by being like-minded, having the same love,*
> *being one in spirit and purpose. Do nothing out of*
> *selfish ambition or vain conceit, but in humility*
> *consider others better than yourselves.*
> *Each of you should look not only to your own interests,*
> *but also to the interests of others.*
>
> PHILIPPIANS 2:1-4

I'd Rather...

by Ray N. Hawkins

I'd rather hold your hand
in the dark,
than
walk in the sunshine
with another.

I'd rather grow old with you
in marriage
than
taste eternal youthfulness
without you.

I'd rather be materially poor
with your love
than
be financially rich but
adrift from you.

Why?
Because
I cannot thrive
without my heart.
You are my heart!

I'd rather share your sorrows
every day
than
laugh with carefree frivolity
in a crowd.

I'd rather be a nobody
in this world
than
famous and feted
never knowing you.

I'd rather die
as your husband
than
live forever
never tasting your lips.

Why?
Because,
I cannot deny
you're God's gift,
his treasure to me.[4]

From Daniel

Before I say anything else, I've got to tell you that I'm not after my wife's pantyhose! But I sure am enjoying her "purse"! Every time I use the case, I think of her and her wonderful sense of humor. I think how wild I am about her and how she's my favorite person in the whole world.

But our marriage hasn't always been like this. We've both had our share of baggage and dark issues. We both had to seek God's deliverance from our wounded pasts. During our troubled years, we could have easily given up on our marriage. I know many who gave up on their own marriages. But now my marriage is great.

If you asked me how this wonderful thing has happened to us, I'd probably have to say I identify with Paul when he mentions "the mystery" in Ephesians 5:32. Really, I think we guys miss out on a lot when we ignore "the mystery." There's a mystery in my wife's eyes when she looks at me. It stirs something in me and makes me want to melt all over her. There are days when the power of this mystery is so potent that I marvel I could feel this way after two decades of marriage. Instead of getting tired of each other, we're straining to move closer all the time.

On top of that, we've fallen into a lifestyle of those "Frito" moments Debra mentioned earlier. Without planning it, we keep doing the same things when we're apart and thinking the same things when we're together. Almost every day now we have numerous "one moments." Then, we look at each other, laugh, and say, "the two shall become one."

I rejoice that this mystery happened to us! I feel like the luckiest guy on the planet. Many times I lie awake at night and think, *How come I was so fortunate to be so blessed with such an incredible marriage?* Debra and I have both gotten to the point that everything else in life—our goals, our dreams, our plans—dim in the glow of our relationship with each other. I have no desire to fantasize about what life would be like with another woman. I'm too fulfilled to even go there.

I'm not saying we've got it all figured out or perfected. There still are days when Debra and I might be exhausted or stressed and find ourselves getting snappy. That's all a part of being human. But since we're one, "love covers a multitude of sins" (1 Peter 4:8). We can't stay irritated at each other for long. Within a few hours we're embracing and pleading for forgiveness.

Ironically, I've heard that one of the worst things a couple can do is work together every day. Some people seem to think that only leads to conflict and bickering and a "you're getting on my nerves" attitude. What Debra and I have found is that when a couple is truly one, working together every day leads to a deepening harmony that only gets better as the days slip by.

Believe me when I tell you that Debra is the best friend I have ever had. Also I have faith that it is possible for this to happen to most marriages—if a husband and wife are willing to make it happen. I guess there are always those extreme cases when the issues of one spouse or the other prohibit the one-couple marriage. But for the most part, I believe you'll discover what we've discovered if only you'll try and if you'll let the Lord begin His miracle.

Prayer Points for Romance

- ❧ Pray that the Lord will show you if you have allowed legalistic marriage concepts to produce bondage and fear in your marriage.

- ❧ Ask the Lord to reveal your strengths and your wife's strengths.

- ❧ Request that God will give you the courage to admit that you need your wife's strengths to balance your weaknesses—

mentally, emotionally, and spiritually. Remember, she needs your strengths to balance her weaknesses as well!

∾ Pray that the Lord will gift you with the ability to accept your wife exactly the way she is.

∾ If you are looking at other women, thinking they measure up to a preset mold that your wife can't fill, pray that God will show you the flaws in these women and how miserable you would be with someone like them.

Romantic Notions

Where has your lover gone, most beautiful of women?
Which way did your lover turn,
that we may look for him with you?

SONG OF SONGS 6:1

What I Did

When Debra and I adopted our daughter from Vietnam, I was required to fly back to the United States for family and career obligations while Debra stayed in Asia to complete our daughter's adoption. Soon after I left Vietnam, Debra flew from Saigon, Vietnam to Bangkok, Thailand. She was required to stay there nearly a week while our daughter's U.S. visa was processed. During that week, Debra and I talked many times. But one time I decided to spice up our conversation and discuss the sensual plans I had for when she returned home.

My Reason

I don't know if I've ever missed Debra as badly as I did that week. I ached for her and for every element of our relationship. I desperately wanted to make love to her, but conversation was as close as I could get.

How I Felt

I felt stimulated with thoughts of things to come and frustrated by my inability to touch Debra.

The Obstacles I Overcame

I wondered if anybody between Texas and Bangkok might be listening in on our conversation. But I finally thought, *Oh well...if they are, chances are high they can't speak English anyway!*

My Wife's Response

Debra has a sexy chuckle that I enjoy. She, too, expressed her readiness to be home.

What I Wish I Had Done

I wish I had realized how stimulating such talk was to my wife earlier in our marriage. Now, I don't wait until we're apart to talk sex to my wife. I continually keep the fires burning by letting her know my thoughts.

Budget Suggestions

The phone call from Texas to Bangkok was costly. Such a phone call can also be free if it's just across town. For the most part, this suggestion will cost you your focus—getting it off of your other interests and fully onto your wife.

What My Husband Does Right

by Debra White Smith

- Daniel never feels threatened by my gifts or talents and doesn't feel the need to compete. Instead, he celebrates my abilities as I celebrate his.

- He tells me I'm pretty even when I'm not dressed up and have on no makeup.

- He never criticizes me in public or in front of the children.

- He never gripes about any meal I fix—even if it's a flop and tastes like something from a foreign planet.

- He always makes me feel good about my hair, even on a bad hair day.

- He gives me foot massages.

- He often joins me in the shower.

- He has never told me he wishes he'd married someone else.

- If he gets blessed in church, he allows the tears to flow.

- He isn't afraid to say "I was wrong" when he was—even when dealing with the children.

- He keeps his promises.

First Bond

Train a child in the way he should go,
and when he is old he will not turn from it.
PROVERBS 22:6

WHEN DANIEL AND I HAD BEEN MARRIED but a few months, I adopted a half-grown kitten from the dog pound. We hadn't had this cat long before we named him R.C., short for Retarded Cat. Believe me, that was the only name that fit him! This feline had some significant behavioral problems that could not be ignored.

In the first place, he *hated* our new preacher! The first time the minister came to visit our home, the cat wrapped himself around the man's leg and began ferociously biting while scratching him with his back claws. We managed to pry the cat from our pastor and hoped that would be the last time R.C. manifested such aggression.

Our hopes were not fulfilled.

Soon after the preacher-leg episode, R.C. manifested his bad attitude again. We had invited the pastor and his wife over for a snack after the Sunday evening service. During the pastor's prayer for our meal, there was an upheaval at his end of the table. The pastor quickly said, "And bless the food—amen!" We all looked up to see R.C. going for the minister's jugular vein. The cat had lunged from the floor to the pastor's neck! The next several seconds were spent dislodging the feline from the reverend and tossing him outside with a "No! No! Bad kitty!" thrown in for good measure.

Not only did R.C. have an unhealthy attitude toward our pastor, he also exhibited bad attitudes with Daniel. Once, R.C. decided to sharpen his claws on our breakfast bar's Naugahyde base. My husband administered a mild swat to R.C. and said, "No! No!"

Well, R.C. ran into the bedroom that adjoined our living room. Daniel and I were watching TV together and noticed that R.C. was under the bed glaring out at us. We laughed and commented that the cat was once again showing that animals really can have bad attitudes. Nevertheless, we became so engrossed in the TV show that we forgot about R.C. After 30 minutes had lapsed, we learned that R.C. had not forgotten about us. The cat hurled himself from the bedroom, dashed through the living room, and neared the breakfast bar. As soon as he got parallel with the bar, he stuck out his paw and smacked it. Then, without even a pause, he hit the kitchen tile and slid his way down the hallway.

Dumbfounded, Daniel and I looked at each other. "I think he was just trying to prove to me that he'd scratch the bar if he wanted to!" Daniel exclaimed.

I'm always about one breath removed from hilarity, so I did what I usually do. I laughed. Never before or since have I seen a cat do some of the things R.C. would do.

R.C.'s recurring antics led us to believe that he had endured some form of negative past. I don't know what befell the cat before he landed in the dog pound and I rescued him. Maybe he was abused by a man who reminded him of our preacher. Maybe the abuse made him resentful and spiteful. To this day, we don't know. I guess only a cat psychologist or God could answer those questions. But even after over 20 years of marriage and a long list of various pets, R.C. still holds the number one position as the animal with the weirdest behavioral patterns.

> *Too many couples marry for better or*
> *for worse, but not for good.*
>
> ANONYMOUS

Sinful Behavioral Patterns

When I was growing up, my mother once told me, "If you want to know how your future husband is going to treat you, watch how he treats his mother." From what I understand, many other mothers have told their daughters the same thing. While this advice is short, it is packed with powerful insight. Whether male or female, we learn to relate to our spouses by relating to our parents of the opposite sex. Just like with R.C., childhood behavioral patterns are so ingrained within us by the time we reach adulthood, we automatically exhibit them.

For instance, in homes where the husband verbally or emotionally abuses the wife in front of the children, the children will eventually join the father and begin to abuse their mother. Many women who are trapped in such situations will learn with horror that the sons and daughters she nurtured from birth can be as destructive as the man who promised to cherish her. Often, when these women leave their husbands and children, the "whole church" will scorn them for abandoning their family, when in reality the poor women are escaping brutal abusers posed as the most intimate of relatives. Sadly, the sons who have learned to verbally and emotionally abuse their mothers will usually do the exact same thing to their wives.

The same scenario applies to women who have watched their mothers slap, disrespect, or verbally abuse their fathers. Understand that if your wife slaps you, she is physically abusing you. Slapping another human being is one of the most demeaning things you can do to a person. Remember, the concepts in this chapter apply to both men and women. If need be, ask your wife to read this chapter with you.

There are also cases where a mother abuses a son. These mothers verbally demean their children and physically or emotionally batter them. Sadly, these mothers are usually acting out what was done to them as children. A son with an abusive mother will develop a critical and closed spirit to her. He'll disregard everything she says and learn to deal with her by spewing back the very same negativity she has dealt him. When he looks at his mother, it will be through a critical and defensive veil. Sons of such mothers project the same behavior upon their wives—even if the wife isn't abusive.

Many households experience all the sinful behavioral patterns just mentioned, but also have substance abuse on top of everything. Sadly, a significant number of children of alcoholics and drug addicts grow up to repeat the addiction or enable those addictive behaviors in a spouse.

Many other sinful behavioral patterns are common among the churched and unchurched alike. A raging parent can also train a child to rage. Repeated threats of abandonment from one spouse to another in front of children will create an adult who has serious issues of fear of abandonment. Then, there are those who suffer sexual abuse and bear the scars of these horrific acts. And there are those boys who watched their fathers have one affair after another in front of them. Some fathers even encourage their sons to sexual promiscuity by example or blatant pressure early in their teen years. The same sometimes goes for daughters and mothers.

Tragically, many upstanding Christian men and women enter their marriages not only scarred from such patterns of behavior, but they also begin living out these sinful patterns early in their marriage. In *Angry Men and the Women Who Love Them*, Paul Hegstrom details the sexual abuse he endured, not from family members, but at the hands of outsiders. Even though his family-of-origin was fairly functional, he still brought significant anger and sinful behavioral patterns into his marriage. He didn't wait long before beginning to exhibit these sinful behavioral patterns. Hegstrom admits he started physically abusing his wife on their honeymoon, although he eventually broke out of this behavior.[1]

A short-tempered man must bear his own penalty;
you can't do much to help him.
If you try once you must try a dozen times!

PROVERBS 19:19 TLB

The Remedy for Sinful Behavioral Patterns

The reason that identifying, dealing with, and finding deliverance from sinful behavioral patterns is imperative to marriages is because the marriage and home are where we live out these patterns. As long as a husband or wife does not address these issues and does not take action to seek deliverance, the two will *not* become one. Furthermore, sinful behavioral patterns, depending upon the severity, can and do lead to divorces.

Many Christians are fairly successful at choosing to exhibit godly behavior out in the world where they interact with others. It's in the most intimate of settings—in the home with the people we are supposed to cherish and respect the most—that these behavioral patterns appear. And if not dealt with, they destroy the very blessings God wants to heap upon our lives.

Tragically, there are some people who don't fully realize they are exhibiting sinful behavioral patterns. They were raised in a screaming, negative, emotionally destructive family, and they know no other way of interacting. However, in the still of the night these people might very well hear the voice of God whispering that they are treating their spouses in an abominable manner. Yet when the light of day dawns, they can plot no way out of exhibiting the same compulsive, destructive behavior that characterized their childhood.

For those who are fully aware of the issues, too many times they use excuses such as "That's just the way I am and the way my parents were before me," as if having parents who lived the sin is validation to continue it. Interestingly enough, the Bible speaks of the "sins of the fathers" in several places—including when God gave Moses the Ten Commandments. Exodus 20:5 states, "For I, the LORD your God, am a jealous God, punishing the children for the sin of the fathers to the third and fourth generation of those who hate me." The application of this scripture must be weighed within the context of the various places in the Bible that refer to the Lord as a just God, abounding in love and mercy. Psalm 103 states, "The LORD works righteousness and justice for all the oppressed. He made known his ways to Moses, his deeds to the people of Israel: The LORD is compassionate and gracious, slow to anger, abounding in love....He does not treat us as our sins deserve or repay us according to our iniquities. For as high as the heavens are above the earth, so great is his love for those who fear him" (verses 6-8,10-11). Notice that this scripture makes reference to Moses and how God made His ways known to him and Israel. Therefore, however we define God's ways, the definition must involve justice, mercy, and lovingkindness. All that is to say, a just God would not punish our son if Daniel and I decided to rob a bank. The way I understand the issue of the "sins of the fathers" is that if a parent habitually lives out a sin in front of a child, that child will grow up and live the same sin. In these cases, God holds the child responsible for his or her own behavior. The Lord does punish this type of generational sin. There's no room for excusing sinful behavior because that's the way our parents were.

After people say "that's just the way I am and the way my parents were before me," the next thing said is usually, "God's grace can and does cover this. Therefore, I'll just stay the way I am." Or, even more tragically, people with sinful behavioral patterns might turn to the Word of God to validate the sin. Too many times I've listened to people quote the following section of Scripture from Paul as validation for willfully choosing sin:

> For we know that the Law is spiritual; but I am of flesh,
> sold into bondage to sin. For that which I am doing, I

do not understand; for I am not practicing what I would like to do, but I am doing the very thing I hate. But if I do the very thing I do not wish to do, I agree with the law, confessing that it is good. So now, no longer am I the one doing it, but sin which indwells me. For I know that nothing good dwells in me, that is, in my flesh; for the wishing is present in me, but the doing of the good is not. For the good that I wish, I do not do; but I practice the very evil that I do not wish. But if I am doing the very thing I do not wish, I am no longer the one doing it, but sin which dwells in me. I find then the principle that evil is present in me, the one who wishes to do good. For I joyfully concur with the law of God in the inner man, but I see a different law in the members of my body, waging war against the law of my mind, and making me a prisoner of the law of sin which is in my members. Wretched man that I am! Who will set me free from the body of this death? Thanks be to God through Jesus Christ our Lord! So then, on the one hand I myself with my mind am serving the law of God, but on the other, with my flesh the law of sin (Romans 7:14-25 NASB).

While Paul's passage aptly describes someone who is trapped in sinful behavioral patterns, this scripture falls between passages where Paul clearly states that we should not purposefully embrace sin or allow it to continue in our lives once we recognize it:

What shall we say then? Are we to continue in sin that grace might increase? May it never be! How shall we who died to sin still live in it? Or do you not know that all of us who have been baptized into Christ Jesus have been baptized into His death? Therefore we have been buried with Him through baptism into death, in order that as Christ was raised from the dead through the glory of the Father, so we too might walk in newness of life....Even so consider yourselves to be dead to sin, but alive to God in Christ Jesus. Therefore *do not let sin reign in your mortal body that you should obey its lust, and do not go on presenting the members of your body to sin as instruments of unrighteousness;* but present yourselves to God as those alive from the dead, and your members as instruments of righteousness to God. *For sin shall not be master over you, for you are not under law, but under grace. What then? Shall we sin because we are not under law but under grace? May it never be!* (Romans 6:1-4, 11-15 NASB, emphasis added).

Therefore, there is now no condemnation for those who are in Christ Jesus, because through Christ Jesus the law of the Spirit of life set me free from the law of sin and death....Those who live according to the sinful nature have their minds set on what that nature desires; but those who live in accordance with the Spirit have their minds set on what the Spirit desires. The mind of sinful man is death, but the mind controlled by the Spirit is life and peace; the sinful mind is hostile to God. It does not submit to God's law, nor can it do so. Those controlled by the sinful nature cannot please God. You, however, are controlled not by the sinful nature but by the Spirit, if the Spirit of God lives in you. And if anyone does not have the Spirit of Christ, he does not belong to Christ....Therefore, brothers, we have an obligation—but it is not to the sinful nature, to live according to it. For if you live according to the sinful nature, you will die; but if by

the Spirit you put to death the misdeeds of the body,
you will live, because those who are led by the Spirit of
God are sons of God (Romans 8:1-2, 5-9, 12-14).

While people's use of the first quote as an excuse for willfully
choosing sin is inexcusable, I have been dismayed to hear people
use the latter two quotes as a platform to claim they have "arrived"
spiritually, have no need for further growth or forgiveness, and
deny they have any chance of sinful behavioral patterns. Neither
stance is a spiritually healthy state. While Scripture clearly tells us
to "avoid every kind of evil" (1 Thessalonians 5:22), we are also
beseeched to be honest before the Father and our fellow man if we
become aware of a sinful behavior in our lives: "If we confess our
sins, he is faithful and just and will forgive us of our sins and
purify us from all unrighteousness" (1 John 1:9).

> *Abuse can be defined as any words, deeds, actions,*
> *attitudes, marriage concepts, or parenting methods*
> *that violate Jesus Christ's Golden Rule:*
> *"So in everything, do to others what you*
> *would have them do to you."*
> DEBRA WHITE SMITH

*The first step to overcoming sinful behavioral patterns is to recog-
nize the nature of these patterns.* Understand that these patterns
are not something you are making a conscious decision to do
every day, but rather patterns you are living out because you have
been trained to act in this manner. I think that's why so many
people who are aware of a sinful behavioral pattern in their lives
identify with Paul when he says, "For that which I am doing, I do
not understand; for I am not practicing what I would like to do,
but I am doing the very thing I hate" (Romans 7:15 NASB). These
people have been trained from childhood by parents or by an
unfortunate set of abusive circumstances to behave and react in a

sinful or abusive manner. For instance, a benign example of behavioral patterns involves the way we speak. Daniel and I have been trained from birth to speak with a Southern accent. We do not get up every morning and think, "Today, I'm choosing to speak like a Texan." We just fall into the same speech patterns that have been modeled to us from birth. The same holds true of sinful behavioral patterns. The reason why it is indeed possible to be unaware of this type of sin is because it can be ingrained in the very essence of our every action. Proverbs 22:6 states, "Train a child in the way he should go, and when he is old he will not turn from it." The opposite of this is true as well. If a child is trained in the way he should not go, when he is old he most likely will not depart from it either—not without some hard work and the strength of the Lord.

The second step to overcoming sinful behavioral patterns is to admit we are trapped in them. Recently, I spoke on this subject at a church that is involved in a growth explosion. The pastor, Steve, an on-fire man of God who is radically impacting his community, shared a story with me after the church service. He said when he was a teenager he worked with the son of a renowned evangelist who had an astounding godly reputation. The son and Steve worked for the evangelist one summer in an outdoor job. For some reason, this evangelist with the "astounding godly reputation" grew furious. His rage increased toward his son to the point that he even threw a sizable wrench at him. In order to keep from getting hit in the head, the son was forced to duck. Steve exclaimed, "If that wrench had hit the evangelist's son, it could have killed him! And right then, something came over me and I thought, 'There's nothing to what this man testifies to in the pulpit.'" Steve continued, "Debra, if he had heard your message tonight early in his walk with Christ, he would have been able to receive deliverance. Instead, he clung to the idea that he was 'fixed' spiritually and refused to admit that he had any kind of sinful behavioral pattern." Steve described the evangelist as one who had come from a terribly dysfunctional home. And while the Lord had delivered him from a whole battery of blatant sins, some of which landed him in prison, he was still living out some of the sinful behavioral patterns from his childhood. I would hazard to guess that the evangelist's father threw things at him. Tragically, one of the earmarks of sinful behavioral patterns can be that the person who is exhibiting these patterns honestly does not see himself clearly or, even worse, uses the Bible to validate the abuse. For instance, in order to validate throwing a wrench at his son, the evangelist could have thought, "Well, 'foolishness is bound up in the heart of a child; the rod of discipline will remove it far from him.' Proverbs 22:15 NASB! That wrench was my rod of discipline!" Similarly, I've heard of husbands who beat their wives with a big Bible and substantiate the abuse by saying they were enforcing her "submissive role."

If you are uncertain that you are marred by sinful behavioral patterns, then get alone with God for 30 minutes to one hour a day for the next several days. Be prepared with a pen and a piece of paper. Ask the Lord to begin showing you the sinful behavioral patterns of your parents. As these patterns come to mind, begin writing them down one at a time. Examples of such sinful behavioral patterns include but are not limited to: a critical spirit toward you and others; a cycle of conflict, perfectionism, physical abuse labeled as "discipline"; verbal abuse labeled as "discipline"; sexual abuse; and spiritual abuse. Spiritual abuse involves:

- using the Bible to elevate the self and demote or devalue others—including children

- legalism or a rule-based relationship with the Lord that will involve hurting other people in order to keep "the rules" that have nothing to do with basic Christian morality

∽ strip-mining the Word of God to prove unhealthy, unbalanced parental or home-life concepts that violate the Golden Rule (Matthew 7:12).

Next, ask the Lord to show you how these sinful behavioral patterns have affected you and which of these patterns you are exhibiting in your own life. Write those down one at a time. Be prepared to be broken, humbled, and maybe even sickened by what you begin to see. After several days of searching before the Father, go to your wife and ask for her side of the story—in other words, how these sinful behavioral patterns have affected her. At this point, be prepared for things to get somewhat messy. As you work through these sinful dysfunctions in your marriage, things will stay messy for a while, especially if your wife agrees to examine her own life as well.

The third step in overcoming sinful behavioral patterns is to accept that it will involve a process of healing and retraining thoughts and actions. According to Paul Hegstrom,

> Abusive situations don't get better on their own. Sometimes people in these situations get disappointed with God. Yes, the Lord can do miracles in lives, but we have to want to change. And when we want to change, then we need God to help us deal with the behaviors of the past. Most of us are so [expectant] in this day of instant everything that we want change now. If it doesn't happen immediately, we have no time for God to make those changes. Most of the time our pain is in the way, and we can't really hear what God is trying to tell us to do. Or maybe God's directions don't seem to make

sense, so we try to "fix" it ourselves. Then we're back to square one.[2]

In beginning the retraining journey, understand that it most likely will be a process. There may be some instances of quick growth and what appears to be immediate deliverance in some areas. But most people's recovery is characterized by a *season* of healing. Sinful behavioral patterns from childhood don't happen overnight. They are taught over years. Likewise, there are times when the retraining process can take a few years to complete. However, just the fact that you acknowledge the issues before God and confess them to your wife is a vital and inescapable step in starting the process of deliverance. Furthermore, in his book *Ordinary People, Extraordinary Marriages: Reclaiming God's Design for Oneness*, Brian Nystrom devotes a whole chapter to "The Ins and Outs of Self Talk."[3] Nystrom states, "Lasting behavioral changes have to be based on real changes in our thinking patterns. Part of this change in our thinking patterns depends on learning about how our self talk affects us."[4] Nystrom goes on to state, "Our thoughts produce our feelings and emotions, and our thoughts strongly influence our actions and behaviors. Our feelings, emotions, and behaviors are the direct results of our thoughts. No one else is responsible for them—we are."[5] (I highly recommend Nystrom's book. If you are struggling in this area, then his chapter on self talk is a must-read.)

For instance, if you are verbally attacking your wife and falsely accusing her, your whole basis for the action might be the fact that you are perpetually telling yourself that you are a loser. This means you strike out defensively. Part of your deliverance will involve retraining yourself not to think in these terms. Another pair of books that are vital in beginning the recovery process are Paul Hegstrom's *Angry Men and the Women Who Love Them* and *Broken Children, Grownup Pain* (Beacon Hill Press).

The fourth step in overcoming sinful behavioral patterns involves regularly encountering God. Once you have allowed the Lord to pinpoint the sinful behavioral patterns in your life, the next action involves taking the time for the Great Physician to do His work. Too many times we approach God in a McDonald's mentality. We sit down for our prayer time, acting as if we're going to zoom through a holy drive-through. Then, we say something like, "Hey, God, give me a large order of healing—super size it, *now*, okay? And smear on a thick layer of blessings to round the whole thing off." Then we zip away and wonder why the Lord isn't answering our prayers. However, if you had a broken arm, I can guarantee you wouldn't rush into the doctor's office, plop down, and say, "Hi! Just wanted to let you know about my arm. Let me know if you can do something for me, okay?" and then rush from the office, jump in your car, and race away. Imagine the doctor, chasing you out of the office yelling, "Come back! Take some time with me! Be still. Listen! I have procedures that can mend your arm. It will grow back together and heal, and you will be able to use it again!" Well, that doctor is Jesus Christ. And the thing that is broken might be your spirit, mind, or soul.

My husband and I both can testify from experience that there's no substitute for being still and knowing God (Psalm 46:10). In my own journey, I have learned to stop talking and turn my thoughts to the problem I am lifting to the Father—whether it involves a behavioral pattern, an area that needs healing, or a problem for which I need a solution. Philippians 2:5 KJV states, "Let this mind be in you, which was also in Christ Jesus."

We are taught that prayer is talking to God. From there, we're encouraged to rein our thoughts in from the fabric of our lives to center on God alone. Meditating on the holiness of God is a worthy endeavor. However, God has taught me the highly beneficial act of laying my thoughts before Him and asking Him to show me, in my mind, the answer to my problem...to show me, in my thoughts, the pain that I am still living with and the means to not react from that pain against the ones I love. However, *this takes time.* You will not receive deliverance until you are willing to *take the time* to allow the Holy Creator to mend your heart. If you can't commit 30 minutes to one hour a day to being still before Him, then commit three days a week to this task. If the only time you have is your lunch hour, then so be it. You will be amazed at what encountering God's presence on this level will do for your marriage. Not only will you begin to be empowered to break free of the behavioral patterns that may have plagued you for life, but God Himself will impart to you a universe-quaking love for your wife that you had no idea could even exist.

The fifth step in overcoming sinful behavioral patterns involves making restitution. This means you go to the people who have been affected by your sin, tell them you have recognized the problem, and then ask their forgiveness. Making restitution is God's way of enabling us to be self-controlled. When I was breaking free of a sinful behavioral pattern that involved a cycle of interpersonal conflict, the Lord would bring people and situations to my mind a few at a time. During my prayer time, God would show me that I needed to apologize for *my* part of a past conflict. Once I obeyed Him, I sensed the Lord's blessing and approval. Then, after a season of intense blessing, God would give me another short list of people that I needed to make restitution with. I went through two years of making amends. After taking care of the past issues in which I manifested this sinful behavioral pattern, I learned that I never again wanted to have to apologize for a cycle of conflict. Therefore, I have done everything in my power to prohibit manifesting this sinful behavioral pattern again. This whole issue of making amends not only frees us from the issue with our fellow man, it also teaches us to stop the behavior.

The final step in overcoming sinful behavioral patterns includes finding an accountability partner or counselor. Daniel and I are accountable to each other. Ironically, many marriage therapists don't seem to think this works. We've also read books by people who say that no couple can overcome painful pasts by working through the issues together; they always need a psychiatrist or therapist. If a marriage is suffering severe physical abuse, then we highly recommend seeking the help of a trained professional. However, we're living proof that a couple *can* work through a painful and abusive past together. We've lain awake until the wee hours crying and praying and confessing and swimming through the murky waters of past hurts, and then finding forgiveness and release in the arms of Jesus. While I don't want to sound as if I'm demeaning the power and necessities of Christian psychiatrists and therapists, I also don't ever want to short-change the power of a miracle-working God in the lives of those spouses who are willing to do the hard work together. However, Daniel and I also recognize that there may be some couples who do indeed need a third party or parties to assist in their journey. In order for a husband and wife to be accountable to each other, they each must be emotionally and spiritually stable enough and mentally prepared to handle the burden of that accountability.

Frankly, Daniel and I each have areas where we have and still do struggle with some negative behavioral patterns that aren't abusive. We have each made the other our accountability partner. If I am struggling, I tell Daniel. He acts like a "coach" and cheers me on while helping me stay firm in other areas. I do the same for him. If he is struggling with an issue, he confesses that to me. I in turn pray with him. We pray together. And, together, we have found that God honors our honesty and our vulnerability to each other. If for whatever reason you and your wife cannot be accountable to each other, then find a mentor or counselor who believes in *balanced* marriage concepts, which includes equal value between spouses that is lived out, mutual submission, and mutual respect. Also, make sure this person will be a strong arm of encouragement and fellowship without condescension or judgment.

> *And we know that in all things God*
> *works for the good of those who love him,*
> *who have been called according to his purpose.*
> Romans 8:28

> *I can do everything through him who gives me strength.*
> Philippians 4:13

You Color My Life

by Ray N. Hawkins

As a landscape artist,
love's brush, paint in hand,
you came into my life.
My heart you possessed.
My lips confessed,
you have colored my life.

Once I was content,
with varying shades of gray,
before you entered my heart.
Your touch created confusion;
your presence, an intrusion,
as you colored my life.

Life has new meaning,
far beyond mere feeling,
caused by love's colors
mixed delicately,

applied patiently,
when you colored my life.

Oh Love,
lose not your paint.
Drop not your brush.
Cease not your touch.
Let my landscape show
how you colored my life.[6]

From Daniel

Earlier in this book I mentioned that Debra and I have gone through some dark days in our marriage. I'd really rather not admit it, but the content of this chapter reflects the emotional wounds I heaped upon Debra from those darker days. It would be easier for me to gloss over some of these issues—pretend they never happened to us or maybe make them less than they really are. But that would not be honest. The truth is, I was an emotional wreck when we got married. While Debra was dealing with her own set of injuries from being sexually abused and some other family-of-origin issues, I was manifesting the traits of the emotionally and verbally abused.

Before I go any further, I want to issue a caution to you. If I had read a chapter like this ten years ago, I would have skimmed through and decided none of it really applied to me. The reason? Because I was blind to the impact of my past upon my present. It wasn't that I was in denial or afraid of facing the truth, I was *absolutely blind!* Therefore, while it would be very easy for you to skim through this chapter and skip onto the next one, I beseech you to take the time to do some intense soul searching.

The other day, several people were talking at church. Some were saying that if their fathers were alive today, they would have been arrested for child abuse. Tragically, many parents from past generations used the Bible to prove that they had the right to verbally, emotionally, and physically abuse their own children. I've come to the conclusion that many in our current population were physically abused by their parents. They just don't understand that the treatment really was abuse or the lasting and harmful effects it has had upon them. Understand that if your parents slapped you in the face, left scratches, bruises, or red marks on you after discipline, or spankings consisted of a battery of blows, then you were physically abused. Also understand that if your parents demeaned you, ridiculed you, or were hateful or mean to you, then you were emotionally abused.

Evaluate where you are in your treatment of your wife and be honest with yourself about anything from your past that might be causing you to act out negative behaviors. If you really don't know if this chapter applies to your marriage, ask your wife. If your wife is telling you there is a problem, *listen* to her! Looking back, I can see Debra tried to tell me we had a significant problem, but I couldn't see it and wouldn't listen. I viewed the issues from my past as too lightweight to have caused any emotional injuries. But now that I have flung open the corridors of my past and faced the truth, I can see that the issues were far from lightweight. No matter how insignificant you believe your past wounds may have been, the impact might be far more devastating than even you realize.

As with anyone who has endured physical, verbal, and emotional abuse, I came into adulthood with zero security in who I was. I felt like I was a loser in a lot of ways. In my marriage, I couldn't imagine why a bright, attractive woman would stay true to me because I believed I was worthless. Due to this woundedness, there were times I blew up for no logical reason. I felt paranoid and jealous and would accuse Debra of things she didn't do and had no intention of doing. Sometimes I was just rude and hateful for no reason.

When I observed our acquaintances, I could tell that maybe there were some people who didn't behave as I did. But I couldn't piece together the reason I was doing any of it or why I felt so driven to repeat the behavior.

Another thing I couldn't understand was why Debra could seem so secure in our relationship when I was so insecure. Honestly, I lived day in and day out for years believing that our marriage might fall apart at any time. There was no rational reason for these fears; they just existed as a remnant of my past.

Debra didn't seem to be eaten up with such fear. I know this is going to sound twisted, maybe because it is, but her security in our relationship bred more insecurity in me. See, my definition of marital love involved jealousy and insecurity. Therefore, when Debra didn't show jealousy and insecurity, I assumed she must not love me as much as I loved her, which only fed the endless cycle of verbal abuse.

Instead of seeing my behavior as verbal abuse, I saw it as showing strong signs of wanting our marriage to work and to last forever. So some of the negative things I did, I viewed as being positive. These distorted behaviors and beliefs only scarred and hurt Debra. She put up walls for protection. I probably would have done the same thing in her shoes. Because I was seeing all this through the "glasses" of my past, I did not recognize that acting out my past pain really crushed areas of our marriage.

Ironically, I did love Debra with all my heart—even in the middle of my messed-up dysfunction. While I really didn't know how to tell her, I still tried to show her I thought she was a queen. Everything we said in chapter 1 is true. Even during our darkest days, I did try to empower her to succeed. And I did shoulder the responsibilities of parenting with her. I treated her as an equal partner. So, I guess I didn't completely blow everything.

The problem is, I would treat her like a queen for a season and then explode on her when my insecurities overtook me. In some ways, I was living out two types of characters. Paul Hegstrom refers to such behavior as a "Jekyll-and-Hyde abusive personality."[7] Because I am soft-spoken and unassuming, no one at church or work ever suspected my problem. Debra has told me she would even despair when she watched how kindly I treated people at church when maybe that very hour I had been less-than-kind to her at home. If you're unsure of what constitutes abuse, look at the chart on pages 66-67.

Even though our past is marked by my emotionally abusive behavior from which we are healing, I am *so thankful* I never physically abused Debra. Miraculously, I've never even *wanted* to.

Love covers all sins
Proverbs 10:12 NKJV

When my wife, Debra, began to follow the Lord's leadership in the marital concepts God developed through her, my healing began. (These concepts are presented in the book *Romancing Your Husband.*) Even in the face of my having hurt her, Debra began to exhibit unconditional love for me through actions and through pouring tons of energy into our marriage. I know through all that time that she was interceding with God for me and for our marriage as well.

The final stage of my healing began during the last big blowup we had. As usual, I had gradually become eaten up by insecurities, and I allowed it to spew upon Debra. I don't recall all the details verbatim, but I do remember that in the past when I would erupt

*Sociologist Murray Strauss states that the true rate
of physical abuse within marriages
involves approximately 50% or 60% of all marriages,
rather than the 28% who report it.*[8]

Varieties of Abuse

∞ *Physical Abuse:* Any violent physical act, including "small" aggressions such as pinching, restraining, or slapping a spouse in the face. Using weapons.

∞ *Power:* Denial of basic rights or personal life. Using legal means of forcing power. Mandated duties.

∞ *Stalking:* Spying. Following to activities. Extreme distrust and jealousy.

∞ *Emotional Abuse:* Put-downs. Name-calling. Mind games. Mental coercion. Controlling behaviors. Conditional affection. Loss of identity.

∞ *Threats:* Threats to end relationship, to do harm or kill. Threats to take the children. Forcing abused to break the law.

∞ *Economic Abuse:* Restrictions on employment and money use.

∞ *Intimidation:* Use of looks, gestures, loud voice, or cursing to create fear.

- *Property Violence:* Punching walls, smashing things, and destroying property. Abuse of pets.

- *Silence:* Use of silence as a weapon. Cannot or will not communicate.

- *Isolations:* Controls what is done, who is seen. Limits or listens in on phone calls. Sabotages car. Frequent moves.

- *Use of Children:* Use of children to give messages. Use of visitation rights as a way to harass. Use of child support as leverage.

- *Humiliation:* Hostile humor. Public humiliation. Criticism.

- *Responsibility Abuse:* Making abused responsible for everything in life (bills, parenting, and so on).

- *Spiritual Abuse:* Use of scripture and words like "submission" and "obey" to abuse. Spiritual language.

- *Sexual Abuse:* Demanding unwanted or bizarre sexual acts. Rape. Interruption of sleep for sex. Extreme jealousy. Treating abused as a sex object.

- *Use of Male Privilege:* Treatment of the abused like a servant. Unilateral decision-making. Acting like master of the castle.[9]

on her, she would put up a wall and retreat. This time, she didn't do that.

This time, I felt her reach out to me. Something was different. I felt as if, for the first time, she looked past all the harmful behavior and saw my torment. Even though I was directing the usual verbal barbs at her, she saw me where I was—in the bottom of a pit. Then she was reaching in to help pull me out. For the first time, I saw the full force and strength of her unconditional love. It didn't matter what I'd done in the past or how much I was going to struggle in the future, Debra wanted to help me out of the trap. For the first time, it was like I saw the force of my own love in her because even though I had been hurting her, I still desperately loved her.

I cannot stress enough the importance of a wife's unconditional love!

That hand Debra extended to me in the pit began a process in our marriage. Many nights we stayed up until the wee hours, talking and praying and working through the mess of our marriage. Debra and I have come to realize that she was so devastated herself when we got married she wasn't able to love on the level she now loves me. Of course, my abusive behavior didn't do anything to encourage her love, either. In a lot of ways, we were trapped in a cycle of dysfunction—one behavior feeding another and another in an endless circle…until God broke in and delivered us both.

What is your marriage like? How are you treating your wife? If your mind is replaying some negative instances involving temper eruptions, rage, verbal abuse, habitual criticizing or complaining, or even physical abuse, then God is showing you there's room for improvement. I pray you'll seek help…either from Him directly or from a trained professional who teaches a balanced approach to marriage and can help you overcome your negative behaviors.

No matter how dark your past is, there really is hope for you and your wife to have a heaven-on-earth marriage!

Prayer Points for Recovery

∞ If this chapter describes you, pray that God will give you a mental vision of what your marriage can be if you will apply this chapter to your life. When you get discouraged while working through these issues, ask the Lord to continually remind you of that mental vision.

∞ Ask the Lord to give you the courage to begin implementing this chapter in your life.

∞ When you begin to shrink away from the hard work involved in change, pray that Jesus Christ Himself will step in beside you and be your strength.

∞ Pray that God will begin to heal any past pain your wife has inflicted upon you or that you have inflicted upon your wife.

∞ Pray that the Lord will begin to repair any rift between you and your wife that is prohibiting your undaunted admiration of her.

Romantic Notions

My lover is mine and I am his;
he browses among the lilies.

Song of Songs 2:16

What I Did

For quite awhile, I've been highly interested in my wife, and I wanted to purchase a romantic game. So I told Debra how much I'd enjoy this, and we began looking for a game together.

My Reason

The idea sounded adventurous and sensual and fun.

How I Felt

I was excited about the idea of a romantic game and the new dimension it would bring to our union.

The Obstacles I Overcame

We discovered that some of the games were just pornography. I didn't want anything filthy or something that featured bad words. I just wanted something that would help us enjoy the romance.

My Wife's Response

Debra was wide open to the idea. She began to look for romance games as much as I was looking for them. Finally, she found a company that makes clean, sexy, tasteful, fun games that Christians can enjoy.* We purchased several. Since then we have enjoyed the games and found that the whole aspect of focusing on each other's interests and sexuality for 30 minutes to an hour makes the sparks fly between us. Debra also likes the games because there are many questions that help facilitate healthy communication. These types of games are a wonderful resource for couples who are trying to rekindle the magic in their marriages.

---

* We now offer these games and other romance-oriented products through our website: www.debrawhitesmith.com.

What I Wish I Had Done

Really, I wish I could have found the games on my own and surprised Debra. But this was one idea I needed her help on since she has a greater knowledge of the Christian market than I do.

Budget Suggestions

These games retail for around $25. If you can't afford to buy a game, then make up your own! You can use an existing game board and game pieces from a family game like Sorry or Monopoly. Then create your own cards and rules. Be as creative and sexy as you like!

What My Husband Does Right
by Debra White Smith

- ∽ Daniel puts a lot of verbal effort into seduction.

- ∽ He asks me what my sexual favorites are and repeats them often.

- ∽ He doesn't take a second look at other women.

- ∽ He doesn't watch racy movies with me or without me.

- ∽ Often, he holds and cherishes me without sexual touching.

- ∽ He doesn't sexually pressure me if I'm sick.

- ∽ He listens to me.

- ∽ When I'm under a book deadline and having to write a lot, he comes and visits me with sensual reminders that he finds me attractive—even if I have bags under my eyes, my hair's a mess, and I never bothered with makeup that day.

Great Sex 101

Under the apple tree I roused you.
SONG OF SONGS 8:5

RECENTLY, I RECEIVED THE FOLLOWING UNSOLICITED E-MAIL:

> How have you been? You would not believe what I
> found but it is true. There is a site that I found for
> people to talk, chat, see each other's pictures, and even
> meet each other as close as next door. But that's not
> the best part. Here is why it's so unbelievable: not all
> the people are single. In fact, a lot of them are even
> married, looking to satisfy their hungriest desires. This
> is "Married but Always Lonely"! You would not believe
> what is going on and what people are saying about this
> site. Check this out!

I usually delete junk mails like this without so much as a thought.
But this e-mail really snared my attention. Not because it touched
a need in me, but because I was made aware of how this message
reflects the truth of numerous marriages. So many people—even
Christians—are married but still feel like they are sailing the seas
of life alone.

Even sex, the most intimate act within a marriage, leaves them
feeling less-than-fulfilled. My husband has told me that having
sex makes him feel as if he touches my soul. I surprised him by

saying I felt the same way. Now, neither of us grapples with lone-liness—not in the least.

I'm convinced that the sexuality of a marriage is often a bar-ometer for the health of the marriage. Granted, there are those occasions when the sexuality of a marriage is inhibited due to health issues or prolonged separations because of such things as military assignments. Aside from these types of unavoidable interferences, the healthiest marriages involve couples who are celebrating a vibrant sex life.

But I have not found that those types of marriages are the norm in the Christian community. Many times people believe that if a couple has stayed together for years, then they must have a solid marriage in all areas. In reality, some couples stay together because that's what they're "supposed" to do, while maybe it isn't what they'd rather do. And sex is something that might happen, and then again, it just might not.

Many elements contribute to the health of a couple's sexuality. As a matter of fact, every chapter in this book deals with issues that impact a marriage's physical relationship. However, there are a couple of intimate issues that especially impact the sensuality of a marriage—sexual inhibitions and emotional intimacy.

> *I belong to my lover, and his desire is for me.*
> *Come, my lover, let us go to the countryside,*
> *let us spend the night in the villages. Let us go early to the*
> *vineyards to see if the vines have budded, if their blossoms*
> *have opened, and if the pomegranates are in bloom—*
> *there I will give you my love. The mandrakes send out their*
> *fragrance, and at our door is every delicacy, both new and old,*
> *that I have stored up for you, my lover.*

SONG OF SONGS 7:10-13

Tips to Increase Sexuality

- Don't demean or belittle your spouse in any way.

- The husband shouldn't adopt any marriage concepts for his wife that he wouldn't want applied to him.

- The wife shouldn't adopt attitudes toward men that she wouldn't want projected onto her.

- Commit to impeccable hygiene.

- Wear clean clothing.

- Shop for sexy bedroom attire.

- Stay in shape as best you can. Everyone is not going to be body-perfect, but even a brisk walk or a bike ride three times a week will enhance libido.

- Eat right. This involves a balance of fresh fruits, vegetables, and protein. If you can find it, organic vegetables and free-range meat are best. A steady diet of junk food inhibits the quality of all elements of life.

- Take vitamins. There are special vitamins now available that help increase libido. Talk to your doctor or pharmacist.

- Talk about stress issues. Don't bottle them up or hide them.

- *Honestly* pray together—not just what you think God wants to hear.

- Work through grief issues. Don't cover them up.

- Break free of sexual inhibitions. They aren't God's perfect will.

- Dare to develop emotional intimacy with your spouse.

- Lavish affection and adoration upon your spouse.

- Talk about past marital injuries, and allow God to heal you.

Sexual Inhibitions

By this point you may be amazed at the quality of Daniel's and my marriage, especially considering our pasts! We certainly are! It's hard for both of us to believe that God took two people with the devastating issues we both grappled with and gave us the kind of marriage we now have. There is no reason we should enjoy the exciting bedroom life and the rich bonding of two souls that we have grown into. Only through God's grace has this miracle unfolded.

Sadly, we have learned that our experience isn't the norm. Instead, a revolving cycle of frustration and detachment often characterizes marital sexuality. A husband may feel as if he has to badger an unwilling wife into intercourse. The whole time, the wife seems to be counting the minutes until this "irritating" activity is over. Even worse, she might believe a lie from childhood—that sex is something "good girls" don't enjoy, so she's always afraid to have too much fun. Then, when the whole thing is over, both spouses retreat to their side of the bed and fall asleep. The next day, the two get up and go about their usual work routine. In about a week, the husband starts badgering his wife again, and the same pattern is repeated. In some marriages, the roles are reversed, and the wife is the one who has the greater sexual need. Whatever the case, if one spouse is having to beg for his or her needs to be fulfilled—whatever those needs are—you can be sure loneliness is a regular part of both spouses' existence.

Frankly, after I wrote *Romancing Your Husband*, I have been astounded at the number of men and women I have encountered who exhibited fear of their own sexuality. In other words, they believed that sex is not something that is supposed to be talked about. No sirree! Not anywhere! Reverent Christians don't discuss sex—let alone encourage couples to celebrate it. If you do, you're "of the devil." Granted, I don't believe that healthy sexuality should be the topic of a Sunday morning service with children in the audience. Even still, I laughed out loud a couple of days ago when I read a chapter in a Christian book titled, "Did the Devil Invent Sex While God Was Napping?"[1] Really, that's the way some people act. In his book *As for Me and My House: Crafting Your Marriage to Last,* Walter Wangerin Jr. states,

> And so there are couples of strong religious conviction whose sexual behavior has neither variety nor ease. The first way in which they practiced sex becomes the only way, because experimentation requires too much attention to the act and to pleasure alone—and to think only of personal pleasure seems self-indulgent. Even to discuss sex for its own sake feels like reading dirty books. They do, then, only what they must, and after some years of the repetition they do less and less of that.[2]

> *Marriage is honourable in all,*
> *and the bed undefiled.*
> HEBREWS 13:4 KJV

Because of a couple of books I've written on healthy romance, I've been amazed at the number of e-mails and questions I have received in the last two years regarding what's acceptable sexually. Many of these are from Christians who are afraid they'll anger God if they get too enthused or free-spirited. Tragically, some basic questions come from people who have been married for many years. I cannot ignore that while secular society may be erroneously encouraging sex with no constraints, the Christian community is still full of people who are afraid that if they explore their sexuality too much God is going to frown. Interestingly enough, "God's disapproving eyes" usually take on the same glint as the parents who convinced them that sex was dirty.

Many questions come from women. (Go ahead and ask your wife to read this chapter!) These women want to know if specific practices are okay. You name it, it's been asked—from the most basic to the more adventurous. The answer almost always is yes, it's okay! The sexual sins the Bible specifically speaks out against are bestiality (Leviticus 18:23), homosexuality (Leviticus 18:22; Romans 1:26-32), adultery (Exodus 20:14), and sodomy (Genesis 19:1-11), which can also result in significant health issues. Anything such as pornography, orgies, watching others have sex live, or bringing another partner into the union would be classified under adultery.

Other than these types of sexual sins, other sexual expressions a married couple consents to enjoying together, in private, are perfectly fine. God will not be angry! Take it from a couple who is having the time of our lives: God created sex! He wants you to be inventive and enjoy yourselves. According to Walter Wangerin,

> *Good,* said God, of all creation, including the bodies of the man and the woman who were naked and not ashamed. *Good,* too, were their desires for one another, desires so strong that they superseded even the ties between parent and child: "Therefore shall a man leave his father and his mother, and shall cleave unto his wife: and they shall be one flesh." Cleaving implies not only a spiritual union, but also huggings and kissings and pressings into one another, the making one of two fleshes. It is most outrageously "bodily." Your sexuality is a gift from God for your own delight. It is not in itself a guilty thing. It is good—and you are free.[3]

If you and your wife have struggled in this area, the best place to start is by committing to discussing your sex life. Daniel and I talk about our sex life all the time—before, during, and after sex. We each brainstorm about different things we can do. We tell each other the new idea, sometimes share a giggle, and plot to try it. After sex, we usually both act like a couple of kids who just got off the most thrilling roller coaster ride of the century. We both describe what we enjoyed most and decide how we want to repeat "this, that, or the other."

If a couple is breaking away from an unhealthy mind-set or fear of sexuality, then the act of discussing sex will begin as a slow and awkward undertaking. A good place to find a sense of security in discussing sex is actually found in the Bible. The Song of Songs, also known as the Song of Solomon, is a whole book in the Old Testament that is dedicated to the sensual love between a husband and wife. I recommend that you read the New International Version, the Living Bible, the New Living Bible, or the New Century Version. Each of these versions is written in up-to-date language that will make the sexuality of the Song of Songs exceedingly clear. Commit to reading aloud together from this book every day or several days a week. Then, pray together specifically about the sexuality of your marriage—that the two of you will begin to enjoy this part of your relationship to the fullness of God's intent. You will be amazed at the exciting journey the Lord will open up before you.

However, don't expect results overnight. If your marriage is plagued by sexual inhibitions, they most likely didn't become ingrained into your psyche or your wife's in mere days. Likewise, they will not disappear in mere days. Nevertheless, the following list of statements and questions will facilitate the process of sexual freedom and communication in your marriage. As you begin asking each other these questions, be open to the conversation that will result:

- What were your parents' attitudes toward sex? Were they appropriate?

- Do you feel that you have adopted these attitudes in our marriage?

∽ Do you want to have these attitudes?

∽ Do you feel shame in relation to sex? If so, why?

∽ If there is a layer of shame covering your sexual self, would you be willing to pray that the Lord will deliver you, then commit to being still before the Lord about this several times a week for the next year to allow Him to facilitate that deliverance?

∽ If you were sexually abused or had negative sexual experiences, are you willing to begin talking and walking through the pain in order to receive healing? And, once again, are you willing to be still before the Lord about this for the next year?

∽ Is there anything I do sexually that reminds you of the abuse?

∽ What is your idea of great sex?

∽ When are you the most fulfilled?

∽ What would be the "perfect date" for you?

∽ What does "getting in touch with the power of your sexuality" mean to you?

∽ If you (the wife) don't have an orgasm during sex, are you okay with that?

∽ What increases your chances of having an orgasm or multiple orgasms?

∽ What can we do together to celebrate our sexual relationship?

∽ What is the sexiest thing you think I have ever done?

∞ Name some nonsexual things I can do that will make sex better.

∞ Name one fun and exciting sexual activity you have thought of trying but squelched due to inhibitions.

∞ Talk sex to me. Describe what you want to do with me and how you want to make me feel.

∞ If I danced for an audience of one—you—what moves would leave you dazzled?

∞ If you did _____ , I wouldn't stop thinking about it for months.

∞ Would you be willing to try _____? If you aren't ready for this now, would you be willing to consider it over the next several weeks?

These questions aren't intended as a definitive list of sexual queries, but rather conversation starters that will hopefully lead to other questions and more insights. Some couples, especially those suffering from significant inhibitions, might want to visit these questions every week for many months until they have worked through all the questions and their sexual issues.

Not only will these questions help overcome true inhibitions and hangups, they'll also assist in breaking away from honest shyness. While sexual inhibitions are a valid concern, some people simply are sexually shy. The sexually shy are often men and women who have kept themselves blessedly pure—no affairs, no adultery, no pornography. Praise the Lord! However, they might spend their lives wondering if there's "more" sexually. The mental process goes like this, "We're having a pretty good time here, but is there more we could enjoy that we don't know about?" The answer most likely is yes. And God has built sexual instincts into both men and women to help you gradually experience new and exciting techniques and thrills, if you will begin to go with the impulses that come to you.

Our experience has been that something new happens nearly every time we make love because we both are tuned into our sexual natures and neither is ashamed of that part of who we are. Too many times, the sexually shy might experience an impulse, but they're afraid to try it. Try it! As long as the new adventure isn't listed among the sins previously pinpointed, it's okay. [Note: If one of you has been sexually abused, I recommend the chapter "Pathway of Forgiveness" in *Romancing Your Husband* (Harvest House) or my book *The Harder I Laugh, the Deeper I Hurt* (Beacon Hill Press). If your marriage has endured an affair, I recommend the chapter "Surviving the Storms" in *Romancing Your Husband*.]

> *How beautiful your sandaled feet, O prince's daughter!*
> *Your graceful legs are like jewels, the work of*
> *a craftsman's hands.*
> *Your navel is a rounded goblet that never lacks blended wine.*
> *Your waist is a mound of wheat encircled by lilies.*
> *Your breasts are like two fawns, twins of a gazelle.*
> *Your neck is like an ivory tower.*
> *Your eyes are the pools of Heshbon*
> *by the gate of Bath Rabbim. Your nose is like the tower of*
> *Lebanon looking toward Damascus. Your head crowns*
> *you like Mount Carmel. Your hair is like royal tapestry;*
> *the king is held captive by its tresses. How beautiful you are*
> *and how pleasing, O love, with your delights! Your stature is*
> *like that of the palm, and your breasts like clusters of fruit.*
> *I said, "I will climb the palm tree; I will take hold of its fruit."*
> *May your breasts be like the clusters of the vine,*
> *the fragrance of your breath like apples,*
> *and your mouth like the best wine.*

SONG OF SONGS 7:1-9

Emotional Intimacy and Affection

At this point you might be on the verge of skimming over the rest of this chapter, or just rereading the first part. You might even be thinking, "Why is this even important? I thought we were going to talk about sex! I just want great sex! Let's just keep up the straight talk about sex. Did I mention that I want great sex?"

Well, believe it or not, this part of the chapter is paramount in your ability to have great sex with your wife. Understand that your wife's need for emotional intimacy and affection is equivalent to your vehicle's need for fuel. Without fuel, your vehicle will not run. Emotional intimacy and affection are your wife's "sexual fuel." If you fill her "fuel tank" full of emotional connection and overflow it with affection, then you will find that your wife will very likely purr like a finely tuned automobile.

On the other hand, what would happen to that automobile if you forgot to pump in fuel, never changed the oil, did nothing to replace flat tires, and left the windows down for the elements to take their toll? You would wind up with a broken down, useless automobile, wouldn't you? The same holds true of your marriage. If you don't lavish your wife with affection and develop emotional intimacy, your wife will view your sex life as broken down and useless. If you really do want great sex, then the next few pages are not optional reading, they are a necessity to implement.

In *His Needs, Her Needs: Building an Affair-Proof Marriage,* Williard F. Harley states that a woman's top need is for affection while a man's top need is for sex.[4] I believe God placed these needs in us to be filled as equal parts of a whole equation. Great sex involves affection and emotional bonding along with the fire of passion. Sex with passion only will leave you empty inside. Furthermore, emotional bonding alone, for most people, doesn't equate with an exciting marriage. Just as it takes what both a man and woman offer to conceive a child, so a fulfilling sex life involves meeting the needs of *both* spouses.

Also, realize that the mind-set "Oh good! I'll do all this stuff just so I can get great sex" will get you nowhere with your wife. For instance, if you pat her on the back a few times, compliment her dress, gaze into her eyes awhile, and then say, "Now, let's go through this list of sex questions," she just might hiss at you. According to Paul Hegstrom,

> One reason women avoid approaching their husbands for a simple hug is because to ask for a hug is interpreted as a signal for sex. When a man learns that a hug can be simply a signal for closeness and that his wife should be able to ask for a hug and not be groped, the couple has reached a new level of emotional bonding. When [a wife] knows that [her husband] loves her for who she is without physical gratification, she feels connected. A man, then, can learn that the greatest intimacy in a relationship is the disclosure of himself. The relationship then becomes safe without the fear of rejection.[5]

There is probably nothing more appealing to a woman than selflessness lived out on her behalf. That's the reason I cooed like a dove when Daniel was thoughtful enough to wait on me with an umbrella at the Boy Scout event (see the end of chapter 1). And that's also the reason Paul propelled people toward selfless love in Ephesians 5. Go ahead and implement these next few pages. Start today! But ask nothing in return. You just might be surprised at how soon *she'll* initiate great sex!

> *Trouble in marriage often starts when a man gets*
> *so busy earnin' his salt that he forgets his sugar.*
>
> ANONYMOUS

I often hear women complain about their husbands' lack of emotional intimacy. They further talk about men as if they are all emotionless rocks with no ability to feel. Ironically, I receive e-mails and communications from men all over North America and beyond who are brimming with thoughts and emotions and insights about their marriages. I often wonder if the wives of these men are complaining as well.

I've come to the conclusion that too many times men are pegged as uncaring, insensitive, and unaffectionate by wives who just don't realize that their husbands never learned the dynamics of a healthy marriage in their families of origin. Or, if the men do have a clue, they don't know how to express it. No mother ever taught them what it meant to be unconditionally accepted and loved. No father ever showed them the way to adore their wives. Neither parent understood what it meant to be emotionally intimate and, therefore, the son is shoved into the world with no tools to empower a healthy marriage. These men's only defense is to wall up, be tough, and act out the behavioral patterns that have been taught them.

When the wife wails, "You don't give me any affection and emotional intimacy!" the husband usually says something like, "Huh?" This only infuriates the wife, and she storms, "You're hopelessly clueless!" as she slams the bedroom door. The husband scratches his head and searches the empty chasm of his heart for some behavioral training called "affection" or "emotional intimacy." He comes up with nothing...only the memories of the distant or abusive relationship he had with his own mother.

To add complications to the whole ordeal, he might also be remembering that his father taught him showing emotions wasn't manly. And the few times he tried to express his emotions, his mother insisted that "real men" weren't tender. So he stuffed it all into a tight closet somewhere in a cavity of his soul and labeled the closet, "Do not open—EVER!"

The same man stands in his living room and stares at his closed bedroom door. He hears his wife weeping on the other side. Not knowing what to do, he plops into the recliner, grabs the remote, and tunes into the latest game. By the time his wife comes out of the bedroom, he's holding a tub of popcorn in one hand and a cola in the other. He looks up to encounter his wife's red-eyed glare. He honestly tries to come up with something brilliant to say but doesn't have any bank of relational experience from which to draw. After strained seconds, the wife storms toward the kitchen. The sound of pots and pans banging reflects her emotional turmoil. The husband decides there's just no pleasing some women, and he goes back to his ball game.

Next thing you know, one of his fishing buddies calls. He decides the fish aren't as cold as the atmosphere around this house, so, he exits for the day. When he returns that night, he'd enjoy a little physical intimacy, but his wife is not interested, as usual.

The cycle continues year after year. The man lives out what his parents taught him—or maybe what they didn't teach him. All the while, he's desperate for a closer relationship with his wife on all levels: physically, emotionally, and spiritually (whether he'll ever admit it or not). But he just doesn't have the tools to succeed. Meanwhile, he watches his wife share more of her life with her girlfriends than she ever shared with him. And he finally accepts what his wife is living out and what his parents exhibited—that a husband and wife will really never fully meet each other's needs.

When a man becomes aware of a woman's emotional needs,
it begins the process of learning how to look her in the eye,
listen, and validate her feelings. She gets his undivided attention.[6]

PAUL HEGSTROM

Some mothers and fathers aren't blatant abusers. Rather, they are emotionally distant. According to Robert Hicks, "Affection for children existed in [preindustrial] families, but parents had to maintain a certain 'emotional detachment' for fear of losing them."[7] Even before I read Hicks' *The Christian Family in Changing Times,* Daniel and I discussed how we assumed parents of the past who buried so many children must have prohibited themselves from becoming too attached to their offspring in order to save themselves the pain at funeral time. Sadly, this method of parenting that started as a means to self-preservation has been passed from one generation to the next in some family units. Therefore, this parenting style still plagues some modern families—not because of a fear of childhood deaths but because of the behavioral patterns ingrained from one generation to the next.

Often, emotionally distant mothers also have distant relationships with their husbands. Therefore, these mothers never teach their sons what my son is learning—how to love intimately and unconditionally. The sons aren't encouraged to hug or hold hands or show affection of any kind with the father or mother. They probably also don't witness their father falling all over himself to serve their mother. Instead, these sons are held at arm's length and forced to mature emotionally alone.

No child can reach emotional maturity alone. Human beings were made to be nurtured to maturity by *both* parents. I get exceedingly frustrated when I hear people insist that either a mother or a father are the primary nurturers. Neither parent's nurturing is dispensable. If at all possible, *both* are imperative for a well-rounded child. If that weren't true, then God wouldn't have given us a father and a mother. That's not to demean the efforts of single parents or to say that single parents cannot successfully raise children. However, in these cases, if the other parent is not available, the single parent should be aware that he or she will need to compensate for the loss of the other parent.

Meanwhile, a son who has learned to relate in a dysfunctional manner at the hands of his parents finds a woman he thinks he loves. She says she loves him, too. Deep in his heart, he is thinking he will finally be able to connect with someone who will show him unconditional love. They get married. And instead of finding that heaven-on-earth matrimonial experience they so craved, they wind up with a version of what they lived out with their mothers or what they saw their fathers and mothers exhibiting before them.

Why? Because, as we covered in chapter 3, we as human beings—whether male or female—live out the same behavioral patterns we have been trained in from childhood. If your parents enjoyed an affectionate relationship full of mutual service, love, and laughter, you will adopt those behavioral patterns in your marriage. If your father treated your mother with respect, reverence, and dignity, then you will treat your mother and your wife that way. If your mother taught you how to unconditionally love with extravagance, then you will take that ability into your marriage. But if you never witnessed these symbols of a healthy marriage and home life, then you will have no resources from which to draw for your own marriage. Instead, you will exhibit the negative patterns in which you've been trained. Specifically, you will project your relationship with your mother onto your wife.

You might be thinking, "Everything in this chapter describes the way it is at my house, but the roles are reversed. I'm the one who has a healthy past, and my wife is emotionally distant." I agree that those situations do exist. I receive communication from men quite often who express this concern. If that is the case in your life, ask your wife to read this chapter. Then, the two of you can begin working through the dysfunctional past, as detailed in chapter 3.

But, if you are one of the men who says "Huh?" when your wife asks you for more affection and emotional intimacy, then I encourage you to ask her what that means to her. Instead of turning on the latest game and finding comfort in the cola and popcorn, enter that bedroom where she's crying, sit on the side of the bed, stroke her back, and say, "Honey, I need you to explain to me what 'emotional intimacy and affection' mean to you. Nobody has ever taught me how to be emotionally intimate. Would you teach me?"

According to Gary Smalley, women have a "built-in marriage manual." He further states that he has "never met a woman who by her God-given nature didn't possess a built-in relationship manual."[8] When your wife begins to share information from her marriage manual, have enough respect for her to do your best to fulfill her requests and suggestions. According to Douglas Weiss,

> A woman thinks about how things are going globally within the relationship. She contemplates the time you have shared together recently and how open the lines of communication have been. She reflects on how supportive you have been, if you have kept your word and whether or not you have treated her with respect. These and many other thought processes influence her feelings [and sexuality] toward you.[9]

Ideas for Emotional Intimacy and Affection

- *Be willing to talk to your wife often.* Tell her what's important to you.

- *Be willing to listen to your wife daily.* Look her in the eyes. Hold her hand.

- *Gaze into her eyes even if you aren't talking.*

- *Stroke her face.*

- *Give her a massage with no sexual touching.*

∽ Dedicate one night a week to holding your wife in bed without sexual touching.

∽ Smile at your wife for no reason.

∽ Applaud her accomplishments.

∽ Turn off the TV and tune into your wife as intensely as you would the latest game.

∽ Turn the kitchen into an oasis of emotional bonding. Join her in the kitchen and help cook dinner or clean up.

∽ If your relationship with your parents was emotionally distant, realize that you are most likely projecting that relationship onto your marriage. Also, understand that your wife probably will feel about you the way you felt about your parents when you left home.

∽ Ask your wife to make a list of the top seven things that would make her feel emotionally intimate with you. Commit to doing one a day for a week. Then start over the next week.

∽ Tell your wife she's the most important person in your life.

∽ Make a list of the ways your wife has positively impacted your life and thank her for what's on the list. Use my "What My Husband Does Right" list as an example. If you brainstorm long enough, you will come up with dozens of things.

∽ Share your dreams with your wife.

∽ Ask your wife to sit down. Kneel before her, take her hand, look her in the eyes, and say, "I would give my life for you."

May you rejoice in the wife of your youth.
A loving doe, a graceful deer—may her breasts satisfy
you always, may you ever be captivated by her love.

PROVERBS 5:18-19

You Honor Me!

by Ray N. Hawkins

Seduced by your eyes.
Addicted to your lips.
Embraced by your arms.
Beckoned by your body.
My beloved,
my companion,
my wife,
you honor me
with your love.

Enticed by your look.
Entranced by your kiss.
Excited by your hands.
Enveloped by your body.
My hero,
my protector,
my husband,
you honor me
with your love.

Faithfulness surrounds our vows.
Mercy shadows our walk.
Openness enriches our day.
Gratitude undergirds our oneness.
My delight,
my joy,
my spouse,
we honor each other
with Godly love.[10]

Special Note: I highly recommend the following two books for helping you deal with issues of sexual sin, shame due to sexually divergent activity, and to develop a broader understanding of your own sexuality: *Sex, Men, and God* by Douglas Weiss (Siloam Press, 2002) and *The Pornography Trap* by Ralph H. Earle and Mark Laaser (Beacon Hill Press, 2002).

From Daniel

I'm just like any other ordinary guy. If I picked up this book and saw the title of this chapter, I'd read *this* chapter first. I'd think, "Forget everything else! Let's just get to the part about great sex!"

However, I must admit that my wife and I didn't enjoy the explosive sexual relationship we now have until we bonded emotionally. As you already know, I had some significant emotional baggage when we got married. So did Debra. Neither of us was able to become emotionally intimate. We both had serious problems trusting and releasing our true selves to each other.

Part of the deal with me involved how I felt about my wife versus my ability to communicate that to her. I loved my wife enough to defend her to the death. I heard about a man who lay over his wife to protect her during a huge Oklahoma City tornado. She lived. He died. He gave his life for her. I would have done the same thing in his shoes, even during the dysfunctional years of our marriage. See, I *knew* that, and I guess Debra sensed it. But being able to freely tell her or express my love for her through open affection and emotional bonding is another thing altogether.

One of the things that helped me was when my wife started modeling her needs to me, as she detailed in her book *Romancing Your Husband*. When I saw her *act out* what she needed, I caught on. After that, I began to really listen to what my wife wanted and tried my best to do what she said.

For instance, there have been times when she's told me she just needed me to hold her at night—no sex! Do you know how difficult that is? Even though I'm a long way from being sexually deprived, lying beside my wife and not initiating sex takes every scrap of self-control I possess. But because I love my wife, I'm willing to set aside my needs for hers. After all, she sets aside her needs for me all the time. There are times when she's not desperate for sex, but she knows I am, and she does her best to fulfill me. The way I see it, that's what healthy marriages are all about—two people sacrificing for each other.

In the middle of this marital journey, I discovered something that surprised me. Once I let the barriers down and learned to emotionally bond with my wife, I realized that I, too, had a need for emotional intimacy. I think sometimes we guys are so out of touch with ourselves we don't realize the extent of our own needs. Sure, I need sex. But lurking behind that need is another one labeled "Emotional Intimacy." And I drink up the open affection Debra lavishes upon me.

After years of marriage and a long journey to wholeness and oneness, I'm convinced we can't have great sex without the bonding of two spirits as well as two bodies. God knows that. That's why He gave men and women these different needs. When I do my best to fulfill my wife's needs, and she does her best to fulfill mine, then together we create an amazing whole.

Prayer Points for Romance

∞ Pray that God will deliver you from any fear of emotional intimacy.

- Ask the Lord to release you from any emotional bondage you acquired from your family of origin.

- Seek God for deliverance from sexual sins committed against you.

- Seek God for deliverance from guilt over sexual sins you chose to commit.

- Pray that God will begin to flood you and your wife with sexy ideas you can enjoy together.

Romantic Notions

[I] rejoice and delight in you,
[I] will praise your love more than wine.
SONG OF SONGS 1:4

What I Did

My wife bought me a digital camera for my birthday. I asked her if she would be willing to give me a lingerie style show and allow me to snap some still shots of her.

My Reason

Like most men, I have a need for visual stimulation. Thankfully, my wife understands this. We also enjoy being sexually playful. This idea allowed us to merge both these aspects. Also, if there's ever a time when I see a sexy magazine in the department store, I'm not drawn to flip through it because I've got my own sexy model at home.

How I Felt

Taking the photos turned into a very stimulating experience. Now, every time I want to sneak a peek at my lover, I can view them from the disk where they're saved.

The Obstacles I Overcame

At first, I was concerned that my wife wouldn't allow me this privilege. But I soon learned she was happy to fulfill me however she could. The other obstacle involved our children. We wound up going into our bedroom and locking the door. A time or two they hollered through the door, wanting to know what we were up to. We told them we were having a "special talk." If you have teenagers, you'll be best served to wait until you have the house to yourself. It was also important to find a safe and secure place to keep the disks/photos.

My Wife's Response

Debra also found the encounter stimulating. She said she felt my total attention and focus and that made her feel wanted, needed, and really sexy.

What I Wish I Had Done

I wish I had thought of this idea the first time I ever heard of a digital camera.

Budget Suggestions

Digital cameras are available for all prices, from around $50 to as much as you want to pay. Our camera is a fairly good one and cost around $300. Your wife doesn't have to buy any new lingerie if she already has some. You can delete the photos after each shoot. If you don't, you will also want to purchase a lockable box that you can hide the disk or memory stick in.

Warning: First, there are some women who wouldn't ever do this under any circumstance for fear of someone finding the disk or memory stick. This is a valid concern. If you and your wife do choose to implement this idea, be extra cautious about storing the disk or memory stick in a locked box in a remote storage space, a locked safe, or another area of your home where no one frequents. This is not a time to be absentminded! Also, since you'll be using a digital camera, you can always delete the photos after each shoot. That gives you a good excuse for another shoot...really soon! Another way to do this is to use a camera that produces instant photos. Then, after you've enjoyed viewing the photos, burn them.

What My Husband Does Right

by Stephanie Attebery

∽ Philip delivers flowers to me at work.

∽ He leaves notes on the bed, in a drawer, or anywhere else, especially when he's going out of town. I leave them propped up in the bathroom to look at while he's gone.

∽ Philip simply admires me "just the way I am." I believe him when he tells me this. I love to hear the attributes that Philip admires in me. It gives me confidence.

∽ He takes me to the lake or park—just the two of us—on a workday when fewer people are around and we can enjoy each other's company more privately. We're away from the phone and TV when we go to the lake or park.

∽ Philip comes to my school during my lunch break and eats lunch in my classroom with me. That's fun and romantic!

∽ Sometimes we spend the night in a hotel in our own town and order pizza. We are able to swim, spend time together, and get away from the telephone.

∽ He arranges for us to take a bath together with candles glowing.

∽ Philip takes me on dates and doesn't tell me where we're going. He always takes me somewhere I like to go![1]

5

Kids and Chores

*He has showed you, O man, what is good. And what does the
LORD require of you? To act justly and to love mercy
and to walk humbly with your God.*
MICAH 6:8

ONCE I HAD A FRIEND WHO LOOKED AT ME and said, "Debra, you just
don't know how lucky you are." She was referring to my husband's
willingness to assist in the domestic scene along with his being a
great father. She was really hurting over her husband's neglect in
these areas, especially his impatience with their daughter. The husband expected my friend to keep a perfect house. Of course, that
was on top of her working in her accounting practice inside their
home and shuttling her active kids all over the place. Furthermore, she was the one who took care of most of the yardwork.

She would get so frustrated with her husband because he stayed
at work all day, came home, flopped in his recliner, grabbed the
remote and a drink, and then "relaxed" for the rest of the evening.
If the house wasn't clean, he figured he was in charge of griping
about it. He expected her to cook supper, corral the kids, and
manage all domestic duties the whole evening. I believe she was
even the one who took on the Boy Scout responsibility. Since she
was an accountant, she handled their family finances and investments, as well as the bookkeeping for her husband's burgeoning
business. He figured that since he brought home the biggest pay-
check he was free to spend his evenings as he saw fit.

Most women whose husbands behave as this woman's gradually start thinking that their husbands are selfish. My friend was no

different. The last I heard, the marriage had deteriorated to the point that the couple could hardly stand each other.

A selfish husband has the opposite effect on a wife as a selfless husband does. As detailed in chapter 1, a selfless husband will make a wife adore him. A selfish husband will eventually make the wife not be able to tolerate the sight of him. I'll let you figure out what that does to the bedroom life.

> *As water reflects a face, so a man's*
> *heart reflects the man.*
> PROVERBS 27:19

The Frontier, the 1950s, and the Present

At times I've listened to some Christian men—regretfully some of them were as young as junior high boys—who were convinced that the Word of God gave them a license to neglect domestic responsibilities. They pointed to verses such as Titus 2:4-5, which states, "Then they can train the younger women to love their husbands and children, to be self-controlled and pure, to be busy at home...." From there, they decide the idealistic "1950s model" of home life is the only God-ordained setup. The husbands come home, claim their recliners, and allow their wives to carry the weight of parenting and the whole domestic scene.

Ironically, the 1950s model of American home life didn't exist when any Bible verse was penned. The Jewish and Greek cultures were highly different from what we experienced in the 50s and now. For instance, young Jewish girls got married at about 13, and many times the men they married were around 30. When Greek women got married, they went into their homes and were not allowed to leave for any reason. Talk about cabin fever!

Recently, an older woman was observing Daniel with our children and said, "I think it's so wonderful the way these young fathers are now taking responsibility with the children." There was a wistful longing in her words. Back in the "good ol' days," many husbands didn't view themselves as a vital part of a young child's life. Oh, maybe they'd take their sons fishing or to play baseball—after the boys got to be old enough. But real men didn't change diapers, warm bottles, clean up spills, homeschool, and tuck the kids in at night—let alone help with the dinner dishes or scrub a toilet.

Well, we don't live in 1950 anymore. Times have changed. And, just as it would have been a grave error to apply the Greek or ancient Jewish models of home life to a 1950s world, so it is a grave error to apply the 1950 mold to the twenty-first century. Those who try to repeat the idealistic 1950s American setup seem to think that God's view of home life somehow got frozen in that decade.

When couples stormed the American frontier together several centuries ago, the 1950s American model had yet to be created! These frontiersmen got married in their teens. Then, they tackled the forest, built a house, and dug out a garden together. By the time they were 20, they had numerous children. Many of these husbands and wives died before they reached 40. The couple got up at daybreak and hit the fields together. Often, the baby was tied to the wife's back or chest. And half-a-dozen kids were in the fields, working alongside the parents. If the baby got uncomfortable, that was just too bad. Many wives were as adept at gunmanship and skinning a deer as their husbands. Of course, this life was leagues removed from the 1950s model. I wonder if anybody in the nineteenth century ever told couples that if they didn't live the frontiersmen's lifestyle then they were out of God's perfect will?

During the '50s era, many middle-class, Anglo-Saxon, urban women were free to dedicate themselves to managing a household and raising children while the husband went off to work every day. Most women were no longer required to work in the fields alongside their husbands—unless they lived on a farm. The farm women were still digging the garden and skinning wildlife. However, most all school-aged children went to school. They weren't homeschooled. That meant urban wives and mothers of school-aged children were home all day long with hours of solitude to cook and clean and do the laundry. And schools didn't expect as many mothers to participate in extracurricular activities as they do now because most moms didn't have a second family vehicle to drive to the school.

Many times, a woman's mother lived nearby. Since the mom's children were grown and gone, the mother would often step into the daughter's household to relieve stress and help with the children. This was especially helpful after the birth of a new child. Since the wife's mother was often there, the city-dwelling husband wasn't required to do anything after he got home but pursue his interests. Often, the wife—who has been home all day by herself or with her mom—might even have some leisure time in the evenings. Some fathers viewed new babies as an oddity that women had some vast, unattainable knowledge about.

But that's not the way things happen now. Frankly, that's not even the way things always happened to everybody back then. This *Leave It to Beaver* setup is predominantly a middle-class, Anglo-Saxon idealistic model. As already mentioned, if you were farmers, nobody left home to go to work. Work was at home, and there was hard labor for everyone, including children and wives. If you happen to be African-American, your 1950s model might very well be different, and it might even include unthinkable poverty. According to Robert Hicks, this *Leave It to Beaver* model "did not figure in the explosions of black and Hispanic populations in the cities. African-American women living in southern states did not enjoy a June Cleaver kind of life. With a 50 percent poverty rate they faced outright brutality."[2]

Or it could be that you were white and your 1950s existence was poverty-stricken, like my father's. My grandfather abandoned the family and divorced my grandmother when my dad was 12. My grandmother had to work in a sewing factory to feed her children. Now remember, this was the "good ol' days" when men or women who divorced their families weren't required to pay child support and nobody was required to pay hard-working women—or African-Americans—a decent salary. Therefore, my father's 1950s model was far from rosy.

There are still scores of people today whose lives don't fit the *Leave It to Beaver* ideal. Instead of a wife having extended family support now, her mother is often working herself or lives out of town or halfway across the nation. This is not necessarily good or bad. It's just the way our lives are. When men and women struck out to claim the frontier, their mothers weren't with them. When the Pilgrims came to America, they left their mothers in England. Or, if the Pilgrims and frontiersmen did take their parents with them, the elder family members often died due to disease or exposure. A limited life expectancy often prevented extended family support.

Even though our modern extended family support isn't what it was in the 1950s, husbands and wives now have the opportunity to bond together closer than couples from the '50s because they can share everything—parenting, household duties, and yes, in some cases, even earning an income together from their home. Husbands now even go through childbirth with their wives, something that was unheard of decades ago.

Interestingly enough, this together pattern might fit closer to what God intended when He placed a husband and a wife in the Garden of Eden. Like the American frontiersmen, they were *together* all day! Neither the husband nor wife left the other to go to work. Adam and Eve didn't have a mom and dad to lean on, either. It was just the two of them and God.

Today, some Christian wives are still expected to live out the 1950s pattern. In other words, they are expected to carry the full responsibility of all domestic and, in some cases, parenting duties. Except now, they might homeschool—a wonderful and worthy endeavor that just wasn't expected in the '50s. This is a full-time job within itself, and I speak from experience. Additionally, many women also generate income by working full-time or part-time. Despite popular opinion that wives work because they're materialistic, often wives work so their families can eat and save for college and retirement. Sometimes it's because the family can't afford $600 a month for health insurance, or the wife's job provides affordable insurance while the husband's does not. Out in the real world, all husbands aren't blessed with six-figure incomes and jobs that provide terrific health insurance. If the wife doesn't homeschool or work, then she is often the taxi for kids in school who have a plethora of extracurricular activities that didn't even exist in the '50s. And if that isn't enough, many women also volunteer at church.

On top of all that, women have pressure from all directions to do a variety of opposing things. Some groups say if you don't homeschool, you're out of God's perfect will. I've seen some people with good hearts and good intentions who have no business homeschooling because they lack the discipline to keep the children academically on track. Other groups say good Christians leave their kids in public schools where they can influence contemporary culture for Christ. Some small, public schools with Christian staff are almost like Christian schools. Others might tear your children down. There are some Christian schools with bad staff that can likewise tear a child down. Some Christian schools are excellent.

Many churches and national ministries hire mothers with children, aged newborn to teens, to work full-time, and in some cases these women are required to work overtime. Then the same ministries and churches who hire these mothers tells wives and mothers it's out of God's perfect will for them to work outside the home. Daniel and I have even heard preachers whose wives work outside the home lambaste other wives for doing the same.

I am not encouraging men and women of preschool children to leave their babies to someone else's care every day all day long. I have chosen to stay at home with my children and have home-schooled them. I'm not saying churches and ministries shouldn't hire mothers who need the income to feed and clothe their kids. But I cannot ignore the guilt-producing, mixed messages so many husbands and wives are bombarded with. Additionally, I believe it's time for Christian ministries and churches to break away from the double standards and double talk targeted at contemporary couples and to become gut-wrenchingly honest. According to Bryan Chapell, his wife has told him,

> Bryan, it doesn't matter what I do, there are people in our church who will accuse me of not fulfilling my proper role. If I devote myself entirely to family care, some women in the church will say that I have abandoned my potential in the workplace and am contributing to the subjugation of my own daughters. If I work outside the home—even part-time—others will accuse me of forsaking Scripture and giving into cultural pressures. For women in the church today, all choices are attackable.[3]

Whatever your wife is doing, if she is like most women today she feels not only overwhelmed by the weight of her load, but she also feels guilty because no matter what she's doing somebody somewhere is telling her she's out of God's perfect will.

After a frenzied day of being pulled in a thousand different directions, today's Christian wife might fall into bed on the verge of a coma. But if the husband is clinging to a 1950s model, he has "relaxed" in his recliner for half the evening and now wants sex. The poor wife hasn't had time to even think about relaxing since she got up at 6:00 in the morning, and it's 11:30 at night. Due to exhaustion, her libido is almost nonexistent all the time. When she declines her husband's overtures, he feels rejected, wounded, and his pride is hurt. When in reality the rejection might have nothing to do with him personally. It has everything to do with the hectic demands on a wife and mother in today's world!

A wise husband lives by Micah 6:8: "He has showed you, O man, what is good. And what does the LORD require of you? To act justly and to love mercy and to walk humbly with your God." He will act justly and love mercy in relationship to his wife and his family. He'll walk humbly with God and will never allow pride to stop him from assisting his wife in any way possible. He'll remove the 1950s glasses and view his wife's life the way it really is.

Instead of placing a guilt-trip on his wife for not being June Cleaver, he steps into her world and does everything in his power to share the burdens of parenting his own children and managing the domestic load. He will act more like a frontiersman than a husband from the '50s. He'll do whatever has to be done to provide for his family. That might include something as glamorous as rolling up his shirtsleeves, grabbing a dishrag, and tackling the dishes. A woman with a husband like that may even have had some time to relax in the evening. And at bedtime she'll be way more likely to welcome her "frontiersman" with open arms.

Her Man

by Ray N. Hawkins

Through the window
she looked,
smiled.
Her man played with their children

rumbling, tumbling together.
Her eyes glowed
from the spark within.

Through the doorway
she peeked,
nodded.
Her man sat with their children
reading, praying together.
Her heart glowed
from the flame within.

Through the hallway
she listened,
stilled.
Her man spoke with their children
fatherly, tenderly together.
Her face glowed
from the fire within.

Through the evening
she waited,
contented.
Her man free from their children,
stimulated, impassioned together.
Her body glowed
from the burning within.[4]

From Daniel

Kids

If ever a man loved his kids, it's me. When they were babies, I changed their diapers, fed them baby food, and rocked them in the night if they were ill. Now that they're older, I love playing

with them and teasing them and tickling them. I find great joy
in parenting those two and being able to make all their special
occasions. I've coached my son's ball team and applauded my
daughter in gymnastics. I go to their piano recitals, teach Vacation
Bible School, and help in the church's Wednesday night program
for kids. I also participate in Boy Scouts with my son and even
take my daughter shopping. During the summer, I'm the father
who's throwing his kids up in the pool so they can make a big
splash on the way down. I have carried half the load in homeschooling as well.

Before I started my home-based business and we began to homeschool, I would take off from work if the children had a special day
at school. Many times, I even turned down significant overtime,
which included some big bucks, in order to be with my children
every night. I really have a deep sense of duty as a father, and I want
to make certain I am in my kids' space as much as possible.

Together, Debra and I make sure our children are in church
every Sunday, that we pray together as a family, and that we teach
them from the Word of God.

With all that said, I will make a gut-level, honest confession.
Sometimes my own children drive me nuts! I know that's not very
glamorous or spiritual, but it's the truth. The deal is, there are
times when I'm exhausted because I've been out with my business for several hours. I come home and Debra's looking frazzled.
She might say something like, "We received three e-mails from
people who want to book us. You need to respond to them. We
received two book orders from the website; one's from Australia.
The kids are due at piano in five minutes. And I have no idea what
we're going to have for dinner."

Then, I walk into the den and hear something like, "Stop it! I
said STOP IT! If you don't stop it, I'm tellin' Mom!"

"Well, you started it. Why should I stop it?"

"I didn't start it! You did! You always start it, and then get me in trouble!"

"Do not!"

"Do too!"

"Do not!"

"Do too!"

And I'm supposed to stand there and calmly be holy? Sometimes I believe two normal kids would try the patience of a monk! I really do! Since I haven't taken a vow of silence, I usually say something really reverent like, "Everybody be quiet *now!*" Then I start slinging my parental authority and send them to their rooms. From there, it takes every ounce of willpower I have not to go into a griping mode in front of the kids about how they get on my nerves.

But griping doesn't do anybody any good. Not the kids. Not me. And especially not Debra. She says when I bark at the kids it makes her feel as if I am barking at her. There's some mystical bond between a mother and her children. While there's a bond between me and my kids, I don't feel as if I am them and they are me. But that's the way Debra says she feels. Maybe it's because of the fact that children come out of the wife's body—whether literally or figuratively (at adoption time).

I'm not saying a mom loves her children more than a father. I mean, when my son broke his arm, Debra and I both were nervous wrecks. We both guard our daughter's good eye because she's nearly blind in the other eye. And Debra and I would probably both fall apart if one of our children were killed.

With all that said, Debra has told me that if I am impatient with the children or don't interact with them, it does something negative to her sexually. We might be enjoying the evening, lightly flirting or stealing a few kisses, with the promise of good things to come. Then, if I am impatient with the children she says it's like she just freezes. She's not interested in sex anymore. She's too busy being aggravated and feeling sorry for the kids—even if they were rowdy and balanced discipline was in order.

The key word is *balanced!* What I am learning to do is to temper my reaction to my children. When I start feeling snappy, I try to get some distance on them—maybe go into another part of the house and do something else. Or I tell them it's time for *them* to get some distance from me. (That's a nice way of saying I tell them to go outside and play.)

Something else Debra and I often do is try to give each other some space away from the kids. Since we're often both home with them every day, this is imperative. For instance, I can tell when Debra's nerves are getting on edge with the children. Therefore, I might take them to McDonald's for lunch. Or if she can tell that I'm really struggling to keep my cool, she'll take them to Wal-Mart with her. This way we don't allow our reactions to the kids to negatively impact our interacting with each other.

Once you have kids, your marriage is never the same. They affect the romance—even the frequency of sex. The days I've been chasing after both my kids all day, I'm exhausted at bedtime! Hey, what can I say? I'm 44, and my kids are 7 and 9. I'm not Superman, you know!

To further complicate things, if your parents had some negative parenting patterns, then you very likely will fall into those patterns if you aren't careful. These negative patterns will sap the romance from your wife. We suggest you apply chapter 3 to your parenting skills as well as to your marriage. Any time you're tempted to be impatient with your children, imagine your wife's face on theirs—even if your kids are at the height of being hard to handle. If you respect your wife as much as I do mine, understanding the depth of how your treatment of the children will affect her will change everything. Go ahead and discipline your kids when they need it, but approach the task with self-control and a lot of love.

A foolish husband remarks to his wife: "Honey, you
stick to the washin', ironin', cookin', and scrubbin'.
No wife of mine is gonna work."

ANONYMOUS

Chores

When I was about eight, my father and mother bought their own business. I think that's one of the reasons I've always wanted to own my own business. I saw them step out on their own, and it inspired me. Anyway, they both worked in the business, so my mother delegated a lot of household chores to us. In other words, I had to iron my own clothes and fix my own summer lunches. Because of this, when I married Debra, I had a reasonable understanding regarding housework. I never considered Debra my maid or anything like that. Before we had kids, we both worked full-time outside the home. I often helped with housework, and we even did kitchen cleanup duty every night together. Even though I did help, the full management of the domestic scene rested upon Debra's shoulders for the first decade of our marriage.

Then she became pregnant with our son, Brett. During the last month of her pregnancy, the doctor prescribed bed rest due to Debra's pregnancy-induced hypertension. That's when the burden of the domestic scene fell on my shoulders. I would go to work every day and then come home in the evening to a long to-do list. At the time we were also raising a garden to cut grocery costs. Since Debra wasn't employed outside the home during this time (she was trying to break into the writing world), she managed the garden and the canning and freezing of the vegetables as well. Now I was left to do everything.

I remember feeling overwhelmed. I would work eight or nine hours every day, come home, cook supper for Debra and me, clean up the kitchen, and then have to deal with the garden. That didn't count the laundry, doing the floors, or the yard work. I recall sitting at the kitchen table in an exhausted stupor while dicing tomatoes to freeze them. That's when a worn cliché tripped through my mind—a woman's work is never done.

Debra was passing through, and I looked up at her. "All my life I've heard that a woman's work is never done," I said. "Now, I know why." We laughed together.

While I thought she had a heavy domestic load then, that was before we had kids. After our son, Brett, was born, Debra stayed home as a full-time mom and house-writer. She still pursued her writing, but she also dedicated much of her time to our little boy. I was *very pleased* with her commitment to our family. In order to help empower her professional and domestic efforts, I would take over caring for our son when I got home. Debra would then do her best to catch up on running the household and her writing obligations. At this point, she was still doing more submitting manuscripts than selling them.

That setup worked well for us. Then we adopted our daughter from Vietnam. By this point, Debra's writing career was starting to take off and I was still employed outside our home. When I got home in the evenings, I would spend time with the kids because I wanted to make sure I gave them my undivided attention for a while. And Debra would take care of some domestic duties and writing. Our kids were just two and four at this point and very demanding. They always met me at the door as if I were their superstar.

I was thrilled to watch Debra's popularity as an author gradually grow to the point that she was also taking on national speaking engagements. I was fine with this, especially because Debra purposed to keep a conservative travel schedule. Then we felt the Lord's leading us to homeschool our children—mainly so they would be free to travel with Debra and me as a family. The homeschooling also landed in Debra's lap.

With all this going on, I soon began to feel as if I wasn't getting enough time with my wife. In my mind, I started doing something really "spiritual." I started griping. Every day when I came home from work, I would wrestle with the kids until I was spent. Then I'd want to sit down with my wife and talk. But she was still up running around doing things. What, I could not imagine! I mean, she was home *all day*, right?

One night around midnight, I heard her beating around in the laundry room. I came to the door and said, "What are you doing?"

She said, "Laundry."

I said, "Do you have to do it so late?"

Debra looked a little frustrated and said, "Well, it's *got* to be done. It's stacked up, and the kids don't have clothes for tomorrow."

"Okay," I said and walked away. Soon after that, I remember doing that "spiritual" thing to myself again—griping! Some days, I felt as if Debra barely had time for me. And I'll never forget the thought that came to me, *If you want more time with your wife, you need to get into her space and help her.* Looking back now, I know that thought was directly from God.

I began to evaluate the after-work patterns I had fallen into—not by any purposeful choice, but rather by a gradual sequence of events. When our children were small, I managed them in the evenings—because I wanted to be a good father but also so Debra could take care of some domestic duties. So for the first time in our married life, I gradually got out of the routine of being an active and vital part of the domestic scene. The Lord began to show me that I was enjoying the TV a little too much and that while I still needed to interact with my children, their needs weren't as demanding as they had been several years ago. Over a period of days, God continued to reveal to me just how much

Debra was doing and that I needed to show my love for her by taking a willing part in some household chores.

So I declared that I was taking over the laundry. Even though I had done a load or two in my day, I had never been responsible for the whole laundry endeavor. I asked Debra to educate me in the great laundry venture. While I didn't expect her to view my doing laundry as anything romantic, her eyes glowed and she thanked me profusely! I thought, *Hey, I can mop, too!* So I did. She acted as if that was just as exciting as the laundry. Go figure! And I thought roses were the romantic key to a woman's heart! I found out she viewed me at the end of a dirty mop with just about as much enthusiasm as she viewed me behind a bouquet of flowers.

I was really feeling a little smug in all my domestic assistance. God blessed me. I got to spend more time with my wife. And our laundry didn't pile up quite so bad. *This is a routine that can work,* I thought.

As Debra and I grew closer and closer in our marriage, I shared with her my dream of owning my own business. She and I began to dream together about the possibilities of my becoming my own boss in a home-based business while I also managed our growing ministry. Soon that became a reality.

From the first day of my new position, I felt as if I was immersed into a whirlwind of activity called "home life." Soon I began to get a taste of Debra's "real world." It was like a zoo, and I'm not kidding. She was trying to homeschool the kids and do dishes and answer the phone all at the same time. That was while she managed the ministry and wrote books, of course. While I did have responsibilities with my business to carry out, I also jumped into the big middle of Debra's world—right where I longed to be.

After a few weeks, I heard myself saying things like, "It's two o'clock, and I still haven't had a shower." One day I looked at Debra and said, "I feel like I've been running in circles all day, and I'm not sure I got one thing done. On top of that, we just cleaned house two days ago, and now it looks like a wreck. And where did all these dirty dishes come from?" As I made these observations, I was nearing the front door to leave on a professional call for my business—and I had to wear a cap because of my no-shower, bad hair.

Debra just laughed at me. "I remember days when you'd call me from work and ask what I'd been doing all day," she said. "I'd say, 'It's been so crazy I haven't even had time for a shower,' and you'd just quietly chuckle. But I could tell what you were thinking—'That woman needs somebody to get her organized.'" Debra then placed her hands on her hips and teased, "You were mocking me, weren't you?"

I laughed and held her close. "You're right. And now I don't know how in the world you kept from going crazy."

After that, I started thinking that it might be good for every husband to either stay home on a domestic-chore mission for one week or several. If you and your wife are both employed, take over the full load of household and child management for a month. This will really open your eyes to the heavy load involved in domestic management. I'm not talking about vacation time where the two of you ride off into the sunset and do fun stuff together. I'm talking about plopping yourself into the nitty-gritty, everyday household life. Since most men can't take off work for a month, I suggest you give your wife a month off from household chores while you do them and still hold down your job. Every morning before you leave for work, ask your wife for a list of the things she knows need to be done around the house that day and then *you* do them! (Be prepared to become sleep-deprived.)

Understand that if your wife homeschools the children plus takes care of the domestic scene—cooking, cleaning, and paying bills—she is performing two full-time jobs. If she works to generate income on top of that, then she's doing the work of about three people. If you leave the weight of the yardwork to her as well, then she's at stroke-level exhaustion.

Next, if you are coming home from work and sitting in front of the TV until bedtime, you're probably feeling fairly rested by ten o'clock. But she's going to be so exhausted by the time the lights are turned out she's not going to want to "party," that's for sure. Believe it or not, there have been some nights recently when the day has been so chaotic and long that I was too tired to party myself. Life was far more orderly for me when I worked outside our home. At least I got a lunch break and two coffee breaks every day! Forget the shower business! There have been some days when I didn't even get a lunch break!

I shared all that to say the following. First, one of the things Debra and I get frustrated over are people who seem to think every marital setup and Christian home should be one, certain rigid way—usually an idealistic 1950s setup, as Debra has already mentioned. Well, Debra and I believe in godly people enough to give them the right to allow the Lord to direct their home and family setup in the way He deems best for them. Some women are great at being full-time homemakers and moms and doing nothing else. In these situations, the husband is the sole bread-winner. Both the husband and wife might love this setup, and that's fine. That worked great in the 1950s as well. However we've heard of some families where the wife is a professional and has significant earning capabilities. The husband has a gift and love of teaching. So he stays home, manages the house, and homeschools the kids. That's all he does. The wife is the sole breadwinner. Since these "one-couple" marriages are based on honest respect—not materialistic, money-based respect—the husband and wife are both content. Some parents of school-aged children put their kids in school and both work outside the home. We know couples who have God's blessings in doing this. Some of them are even fortunate enough to work at the school where their children attend.

But none of the previous marital setups would suit Debra or me. Neither of us would find fulfillment staying home full-time and not generating an income. Debra says if she didn't write her brain would go into overdrive and fry. If I stayed home all the time, I'd get cabin fever and die. And for various reasons, there have been seasons when neither of us wanted to place our children into a school. We preferred homeschooling them. By the same token, neither of us wants to drive off to a job and stay every day, all day long and leave the other one at home. We love being self-employed in our home. We are enamored with each other and want to be together!

However, Debra and I both know every couple on the planet cannot follow our marital setup, which is similar to the model from the early 1800s when couples farmed together. It's also closer to the Garden of Eden model than the 1950s model. Obviously, we aren't farming, but we are *working together*. We are both running home-based businesses and are sharing everything. We each carry half the load in all aspects of parenting our children. We each carry about half the domestic load. We even spend close to the same number of hours dedicated to generating an income. But we're both doing that from home, so we're with our kids most of the time. Then, when we travel for our ministry, that is a together experience as well: Debra speaks and Debra and I sing together. We understand that while many couples may *want* to work together from home as we are, few get to. Furthermore, if every Christian couple followed our model, society would be void of Christian surgeons, firefighters, pilots, teachers, and professors, just to name a few. The last I checked, you can't perform surgeries, put out fires, or fly airplanes from a home office.

What I want to do is encourage you, as one husband to another, to get into your wife's domestic space, however that best suits your lifestyle and home setup. If your job is strenuous and your wife is a full-time homemaker and mom, it might mean that you willingly and cheerfully donate one Saturday a month to filling your wife's "honey-do" list. If your wife is homeschooling and mothering and working from the home, it might mean that you do like I did and declare that you're taking over a few major chores. If you and your wife both have high-impact careers and no kids, it might mean that you hire a housekeeper to come in once a week and take care of everything. (We have had a housekeeper before as well.) You can also take a significant amount of laundry to the cleaners and have them do that chore. If you're grappling with exactly what to do, then ask your wife and consult the Lord. Between the three of you, you'll be able to determine what is right for you and your home.

Take it from a real man and football fan, laundry and other domestic chores are really not that hard to do. My manhood is not compromised. I'm still all guy. My wife still thinks I'm hot. Her respect for me has never been higher. The chores are just time-consuming, that's all. But when you see the appreciation in your wife's eyes, you'll understand that it's time well-spent.

Prayer Points for Romance

- ∞ Ask the Lord to temper any impatience you feel with your children.

- ∞ Pray that God will show you areas where you can spend more time with and be a better father to your kids.

- ∞ Pray that the Lord will open your eyes to the domestic workload your wife is carrying.

- ∞ Ask the Lord to give you the strength to pour yourself into your wife's world—even if that means giving up a favored TV show or a hobby.

- ∞ Pray that God will deliver you from any unhealthy attitudes concerning domestic duties, such as "real men don't vacuum."

Romantic Notions
by Ronnie Johnson

*Listen! My lover is knocking: Open to me, my sister,
my darling, my dove, my flawless one.*
SONG OF SONGS 5:2

What I Did

I turned our home into a romantic getaway at lunchtime. As proprietor of "The Lover's Dining Room," I designed a menu titled "Me-N-U," which I printed on red paper with romantic names for each item on the menu. As chef, I had prepared iced tea, Cornish game hens, wild rice, broccoli, rolls, along with gelatin for dessert. As maître d', I made sure we had the best table in the house, complete with candles and teddy bear as a centerpiece. As waiter, I poured my wife tea, brought her food, and even placed the napkin (a cloth one) in her lap. As husband, I kissed her between each serving!

My Reason

We have a standing lunch date once a week. We usually go to a restaurant for their lunch special. I wanted to do something to make our entire lunch special.

How I Felt

It was fun, and I felt creative. I kept the whole thing a secret so that I could surprise my wife with the extra effort.

The Obstacles I Overcame

I was waiting at noon when my wife got off for lunch. I hurried her into the car and told her we had a 12:15 lunch reservation at a very special place. She only had an hour off from work for lunch, and the drive home took ten minutes, so our lunch was a little rushed.

If you work during your wife's office hours, you will probably have to take some extra time off.

My Wife's Response

She was pleased and appreciative that I had planned and prepared everything all by myself. She said she was disappointed to have to hurry back to work.

What I Wish I Had Done

I just wish we had more time.

Budget Suggestions

If you like to cook, you can do exactly like I did. Depending on your budget, you can make the meal more or less extravagant. If you don't know how to cook, pick up a complete lunch at a deli or restaurant. Many department stores now have roasted chicken and a variety of salads. You can easily purchase the whole meal for $10 or less, if you watch your pennies.[5]

What My Husband Does Right
by Debra White Smith

∞ Daniel consults me on every major decision, including his business issues, and often does what I suggest. (I return the consideration.)

∞ He automatically takes care of things in his areas of expertise (such as car and house maintenance) without my having to ask him to do it.

∞ Brazil nuts are my favorite. He digs out the Brazil nuts from the can of mixed nuts just for me.

∞ In all the years I've known Daniel, I've never heard him utter one curse word.

∞ He always insists that I take the first bite of his ice cream.

∞ We've always owned two vehicles. He has always insisted that I drive the newest one.

∞ Daniel drops everything and comes to my rescue during any crisis, such as a flat tire, and he never complains.

∞ He has never hit me or threatened to hit me with actions or words.

The Truth About Love

And the man said, "This is now bone of my bones, and flesh of my flesh;
she shall be called Woman, because she was taken out of Man."
For this cause a man shall leave his
father and his mother, and shall cleave to his wife;
and they shall become one flesh.
GENESIS 2:23-24 NASB

From Daniel

I AM INSERTING A NOTE HERE TO PREPARE you for this chapter. Debra and I both agree that this chapter might challenge much of what is taught on marriage in some parts of the church. As a man, I understand that you might be tempted to cling to what you have been taught, maybe even from childhood, and dismiss these new insights. However, I'm asking you to read this chapter—even the parts that make you uncomfortable. Stick it out to the very end and seriously consider everything we say.

Also, understand that this chapter is but one building block among other healthy, balanced marriage concepts that this book and Debra's book *Romancing Your Husband* feature. The kind of marriage Debra and I have doesn't happen overnight, and it doesn't happen by applying one concept and ignoring others. However, issues like the ones addressed in this chapter are important to creating a heaven-on-earth marriage.

Also, as one man to another, I want to let you know that Debra radically lives Jesus in our marriage. Because we live the concepts embraced in this chapter, neither one of us is afraid of being lorded over or bossed around. In Debra's case, her servant's heart pours out all over me and the kids. She does everything possible to empower me, and I do the same for her. I have never felt more respected and loved in my whole life. There have been times when she has actually kissed my feet! I was humbled and a little embarrassed. But she did it because she's intimate with Jesus, and she lives what this chapter says. I'll admit that some of this is a challenge because it involves really allowing the Lord to purify our hearts to the point that we can get a clear view of Jesus and what He is really all about. In our humanity, that is never an effortless journey. It's way easier to stick to the status quo and float along in mediocrity.

With all that said, I invite you to consider one question while you are reading this chapter: What kind of marriage do you want? Do you want what Debra and I have grown into—a blazing love affair with a wife who is free to embrace her own sexuality and unleash that upon you? Do you want your wife to be your enchantress, your mistress, your dream-lover—not just once in awhile, but as a lifestyle? Most husbands answer, "*Yes!*" Well, then, I have another question for you: Have the marriage concepts you embraced given you that kind of relationship?

Mutual Love, Respect, and Submission

Recently, Daniel and I were preparing to fly to a marriage conference in North Carolina. I was flying into the Dallas/Ft. Worth airport from a trip to Canada and meeting him and the kids there for our flight to North Carolina. While Daniel was waiting for me to meet him, he saw a sobbing woman who appeared to have just received the gravest news. So intense was her emotion that Daniel wondered if she'd just learned her child had died. Tears streamed down her crumpled face as she fought to control her emotions. Her clothing, head covering, and swarthy complexion indicated that she was from the Middle East.

Daniel, ever the compassionate man, was deeply disturbed by her brokenness and tears. He was even tempted to approach her and ask if there was anything he could do to help her. Then, through the harried crowd, he noticed a Middle Eastern man about eight feet ahead of the crying woman. Soon he realized by the woman's close adherence to this man's path that she was probably his wife. Daniel immediately understood there was nothing he could do to help the poor lady. Even if he tried, he suspected her husband would probably be highly offended that another male had approached his wife—despite the fact that the husband was doing nothing to comfort his spouse.

Daniel's level of frustration rose as he realized the husband had no regard for his wife's feelings. Even worse, he began to wonder if the husband may have been responsible for her weeping. Instead of consoling her, the man had literally turned his back to her and essentially said, "I don't give one care about what's going on with you or how you feel. You are to follow me, whether you like it or not!"

Daniel didn't tell me this story until after the marriage conference, when we were in the hotel room with our kids. Over takeout pizza and salad, he shared his frustration. The actions of that husband are so far removed from Daniel's mind that he couldn't believe a man could be so cold and insensitive, even considering Middle Eastern cultural norms.

> *It's impossible to truly cherish or cleave to a wife*
> *when she's walking behind you.*
> DEBRA WHITE SMITH

When I was growing up in a mainline denomination, my pastor father encouraged me to believe that I was an individual, crafted in the image of God. I entered my adult years believing that I was free to celebrate my spiritual gifts in my home, in the church, and in the community. Fortunately, I married a man who believed the exact same thing and has done everything in his power to enable me.

Once I arrived in my adult years, I gradually became aware that this isn't always the case. Some people are taught that God intends a wife to be subordinated to her husband in her marriage and in her home. This doctrine is so strongly spoken by respected male and female leaders—locally, regionally, and nationally—that I began to wonder if it must be true; that perhaps my parents just forgot to tell me. I didn't ponder that long before God pulled me back to my roots and back to the healthy things my parents did teach. As a young adult, I fully rejected the one-sided teaching that made me feel inferior and wounded my spirit. Soon I was engulfed in overwhelming gratitude that my parents had the fortitude and spiritual insight to teach me as they did. Furthermore, I overflowed with appreciation for my husband's equally healthy attitude.

As my spiritual journey continued, I sought the Lord with my whole heart. I began to dig into the Bible with both hands and spiritually devour the Word of God, to digest the teachings of Christ. I flung myself at the feet of the Holy Creator and asked Him to give me the mind of Christ, to engulf me with His unconditional love, to give me His heart for my marriage.

From that journey came the realization that I, as a godly woman, should be radically romancing my husband and pouring vital energies into meeting all of Daniel's needs. I also realized that if I was going to live Christ, there was no place within my heart for the "down-with-men" mentality that some Christian women adopt from our secular society. There's nothing holy about demeaning the opposite sex, whether the negativity comes from women or men.

But also out of my journey came a gradual realization that sometimes Christians use the Word of God to elevate and empower themselves, rather than elevating and empowering others and, therefore, living Jesus Christ. Whether we are male or female, until we have had a complete reversal of every self-centered thought, we have yet to see the full heart of Christ.

To have a marriage filled with love and passion, both partners must be willing to elevate and empower each other. In a heaven-on-earth marriage, there is no room for self-centeredness or self-promotion. Husband and wife must do as Paul advocates: "Submit to one another out of reverence for Christ" (Ephesians 5:21). Unfortunately, this isn't what has usually been taught in the Christian church.

Isolate and Destroy

Throughout history some people have misused the Word of God to further sin-based concepts, elevate the self, and promote bondage and pain rather than freedom and life—not only in marriage, but in other areas of relationship. A person who purposely does this must first decide what he or she is going to believe. Next, he or she must scour the Bible for the key scriptures that support that belief. Then the individual must lift those scriptures out of the Bible and string them together with commentary that logically links them. During this process, the "scholar" must turn a blind eye to any key Bible passages that refute his or her concepts. Ultimately, Jesus Christ Himself and everything He taught can be neglected or minimized. This method is referred to by Jack and Judy Balswick in *The Family: A Christian Perspective on the Contemporary Home* as strip mining:

> A common approach is to pick out the key verses from the various scriptural passages dealing with the family. These verses are then arranged as one would arrange a variety of flowers to form a pleasing bouquet. However, such a use of Scripture presents problems when Christians come up with different bouquets of verses and then disagree as to what the Bible has to say about

> family life. This method of selecting certain verses about the family can be compared to strip mining. Ignoring the historical and cultural context, the strip miner tears into the veins of Scripture, throws the unwanted elements aside, and emerges with selected golden nuggets of truth. Too often, searching for God's truth about the family ends up with truth that conforms to the preconceived ideas of the miner doing the stripping.[1]

Of course, many Bible scholars and believers do not treat Scripture this way. Nevertheless, some Christians do embrace bad scholarship methods and, in turn, embrace bondage-producing concepts on marriage and family, church life, and even the character of God. I call this strip-mining scholarship the "Isolate and Destroy" method. When you isolate Scripture, you can destroy relationships.

United States history is a prime example of this. A race of people used the Bible to insist that they were "superior" to another race and, therefore, were licensed by God to put the "inferior" race into slavery. In a movie on slavery there was a highly disturbing scene where a slave owner orders his slave to be brutalized. With the sounds of the slave's agonized cries ripping across the land, the slave owner goes into his parlor, opens the Word of God, and calmly begins to read. Too often, this was probably the case. When it came to the issue of slavery, whole denominations approved and applauded the horrific practice. Some church groups even split because there were "troublemakers" who insisted that slavery could never be in line with the heart of Christ.

Those who were convinced that God smiled on slavery claimed things such as, "My Bible teaches that the Lord approves of slavery." From there, they would begin the "Isolate and Destroy" method of research by citing key scriptures that affirmed this sin.

They would point to Leviticus 25:44, "As for your male and female slaves whom you may have—you may acquire male and female slaves from the pagan nations that are around you" (NASB). Then they would say something like, "Since Africa is a pagan nation, God approves of my owning slaves. Paul even supports slavery. Look at Ephesians 6:5, 'Slaves, be obedient to those who are your masters according to the flesh, with fear and trembling, in the sincerity of your heart, as to Christ' (NASB). See there! God approved it in the Old Testament. Paul approves it in the New Testament. Therefore, it is perfectly God-anointed for me to own slaves." Sadly, I've run across people in churches, even in the twenty-first century, who would probably still be slave-owners and probably still use the Bible to prove it was okay if there had never been a civil war.

The problem with this self-elevating thought process is that in order to use the Bible to prove that God favors slavery, a person has to ignore many of the teachings of Jesus and Paul. In Matthew 7:12, Jesus Christ said, "Therefore, however you want people to treat you, so treat them, for this is the Law and the Prophets" (NASB). I can guarantee that not one slave owner wanted to *be* a slave! Jesus Christ taught, "A new commandment I give to you, that you love one another even as I have loved you, that you also love one another" (John 13:34 NASB). Purchasing a person, tearing him or her away from family, and forcing him or her to labor as a piece of property is the antithesis of Christ's love. Paul himself wrote, "Submit to one another out of reverence for Christ" (Ephesians 5:21). Not only is there nothing loving about owning slaves, there is nothing submissive about owning slaves, either. Instead, the slave owner forces the slave to submit to him or her.

Another means people used to validate owning slaves was by viewing Africans as animals or, at best, lesser human beings. Some people even went so far as to suggest that Africans didn't have souls. This of course, ranked them as nothing more than work horses. Therefore, when Jesus said, "Love each other as I have loved you" (John 15:12), slavery supporters could say something like, "That doesn't apply to Africans because they are animals, not true people." Thankfully, most Christians now agree that God did not approve of slavery or these nauseating attitudes.

In the same way, when a man, church, or ministry uses the Word of God to demean, demote, or limit women, there's probably strip mining in progress. And an unhealthy view of the worth of women, including wives, often accompanies this defective scholarship. Whether these actions or attitudes are subtle or blatant, the women are negatively affected. Subordinated women have been taught that they should suppress their spiritual growth, their opinions, and their personalities to conform to an unhealthy view of submission. Depending on the level of restraint involved in the unbalanced concepts, this suppression is sometimes obvious and sometimes so subtle it's difficult to recognize. Women can't be spiritually, mentally, and emotionally suppressed without it affecting every part of them—including their sexuality. Subordinated wives will undoubtedly "give in" when their husbands express a need for sex because that's their duty and they are supposed to be submissive. Most subservient wives *never* plot to create a sizzling love affair in their marriages. Instead of embracing the beauty of their sexuality and unleashing that upon their husbands in a healthy expression of adoration and love, such women essentially become sexually apathetic or inactive.

So their husbands oftentimes lie awake at night, despairing that their wives will never fully meet their needs. Sure, sex might happen regularly but the act is far from the dynamic, exhilarating, mind-blowing experience that it can be. These husbands may even resign themselves to believing their wives just aren't capable of satifying their needs. From there, the husbands become vulnerable to sexual sin.

Today, the Christian divorce rate is higher than the non-Christian divorce rate in some areas of the country. Not every Christian divorce is linked to the misuse of Scripture against wives, but erroneous marriage concepts, such as one-sided submission, can be a major contributing factor to many Christian divorces.

> *The Bible is a collection of checks and balances.*
> *When you ignore the checks you lose the balance.*
> DEBRA WHITE SMITH

Embrace and Thrive

The acid test of whether or not God really approves of marital concepts, parenting concepts, or even theology lies in how the teachings measure up to what Jesus spoke. As Christians, we believe that Jesus was God in the flesh. We believe that He was born of a virgin and came to earth as our Savior. He is our constant guide; He now lives in our hearts. While the Bible is God's irrefutable spiritual authority for our lives, we must sift every scripture through what Christ said. Then, and only then, do we find balance and the freedom to develop a heaven-on-earth marriage. When *both spouses* embrace Jesus' teachings and die to themselves, marriages thrive!

For generations some people have isolated such verses as Genesis 3:16 as a gauge for what a Christian marriage should be. After Adam and Eve sinned in the Garden of Eden, God spoke the consequences of sin to both of them. He first told Eve she would have pain in childbirth. The Lord further said to Eve, "Your desire will be for your husband, and he will rule over you" (Genesis 3:16). Some well-meaning men and women lift this verse out of the Bible as validation that the husband's role is to rule or "be over" the wife. They say that this is God's curse upon Eve. But is that what husbands want? They want their wives to view them and their relationship as part of a curse? Surely not! Women who view their husbands as part of a curse eventually resent and distrust them. In such marriages, honest romance is nonexistent.

Adam didn't want to rule Eve before sin entered his heart. That is what the carnal (sinful) nature does. It wants to rule—whether male or female. It wants to kill—through a blatant murder, as Cain killed Abel, or through "small deaths," orchestrated by destroying the self-esteem of others by telling them they aren't as important as "I am." Jesus Christ came and repeatedly spoke out against ruling or elevating the self—whether you are male or female—in any circumstance in life: "Neither be ye called masters: for one is your Master, even Christ. But he that is greatest among you shall be your servant. And whosoever shall exalt himself shall be abased; and he that shall humble himself shall be exalted" (Matthew 23:10-12 KJV). The New American Standard Bible states the same verse this way: "And do not be called leaders; for One is your Leader, that is, Christ. But the greatest among you shall be your servant. And whoever exalts himself shall be humbled; and whoever humbles himself shall be exalted."

If you want to know how to revolutionize your marriage, use the "Embrace and Thrive" method of biblical scholarship. *Embrace Jesus and thrive! Start with Jesus first!* Read every word He spoke. Read His words over and over again until they are engraved upon your mind and your heart. Once you develop this radical intimacy with Christ and His words, you will understand the heart of Christ because His heart will become *your* heart.

Within this realm, you will see that there is never holy approval of subordinating another person due to gender, race, or even economic issues. Whether we are male or female, black or white, rich or poor, the only person Christ calls us to subordinate is ourselves:

> ∞ "Also a dispute arose among them as to which of them was considered to be greatest. Jesus said to them, 'The kings of the Gentiles lord it over them; and those who

exercise authority over them call themselves Benefactors. But you are not to be like that. Instead, the greatest among you should be like the youngest, and the one who rules like the one who serves. For who is greater, the one who is at the table or the one who serves? Is it not the one who is at the table? But I am among you as one who serves'" (Luke 22:24-27).

∞ "An argument started among the disciples as to which of them would be the greatest. Jesus, knowing their thoughts, took a little child and had him stand beside him. Then he said to them, 'Whoever welcomes this little child in my name welcomes me; and whoever welcomes me welcomes the one who sent me. For he who is least among you all—he is the greatest'" (Luke 9:46-48).

∞ "And just as you want people to treat you, treat them in the same way" (Luke 6:31 NASB; see also 18:14; Matthew 19:30; and John 15:9-15,17).

Paul and Marriage

You may be thinking. "Okay. I see what you're saying, but how does what Paul wrote fit this idea that there is mutual love, respect, and submission?" Great question! Traditionally, Paul's teachings have been used to support hierarchical marriage—just as he was interpreted to support slavery. However, this view of marriage that has been traditionally derived from Paul's teachings loses credence when Scripture is approached with an overall recognition of the general teachings of Christ and an understanding of Paul's total message on marriage and the body of Christ. In order to support the hierarchical marriage, Bible interpreters must focus on specific words or passages to the exclusion of others that talk about mutual respect and submission, being one in Christ, and so forth.

If we were to apply this approach to sports, the problem instantly becomes obvious. If a coach began to concentrate on one player or position to the exclusion of the others, the team would never succeed. Good coaches understand that no position on a ball team is more inportant than another. Each person plays his part in the working of the whole unit. If a coach leaves one player off or decides the third baseman is more important than the first baseman, then he'd have an unbalanced team. The first baseman would begin to resent the third baseman and the coach. Attitudes would sour. The team wouldn't win many games.

But let's just say the coach decided the second-base position was the most important of any on the field. So he resolves that since that spot is the most valuable, he'll have all the players gang up there. He has the whole ball team in a cluster not far behind the pitcher's mound. But nobody is on that mound to pitch the ball. There's no catcher, no outfielders, and no shortstop. All players are at second base. While the opposing team members might have a horrid time getting past second base—that is, if they were ever pitched a ball to actually hit—once they maneuvered past second they'd be free to trot to homeplate and score run after run.

I think you'll have to agree that this is a ridiculous way to play baseball.

Now, if we approach the Bible like that, we run into similar problems. If we isolate one word or one section in the Bible to prove unbalanced marriage concepts, the marriage will die. Sometimes it's hard to spot a dead marriage because Christians are notorious for putting on positive fronts. These people worry about what people will think, especially since they appear to have it all together. Silently, they observe other couples who seem to be thriving while embracing these erroneous concepts, and they're intimidated into believing they are uniquely dysfunctional. Ironically, they don't understand that those other couples have dead marriages, too, but they're afraid to admit it. Some of these couples might even teach marriage classes or conferences or be in charge of major ministries. The *last* thing they want to do is admit that their concepts don't work, especially since Paul has been traditionally inerpreted in a way that "proves" their marital setup is correct.

The apostle Paul's thoughts are crucial to a solid biblical understanding of marriage. Unfortunately, some of his main concepts have been lifted out of the context of other biblical principles and the teachings of Christ. Let's look at one passage that has often been misconstrued to teach hierarchal marriage.

Ephesians 4:32–5:1-2,21-33

> [4:32] Be kind and compassionate to one another, forgiving each other, just as in Christ God forgave you. [5:1] Be imitators of God, therefore, as dearly loved children [2] and live a life of love, just as Christ loved us and gave himself up for us as a fragrant offering and sacrifice to God.... [21] Submit to one another out of reverence for Christ. [22] Wives, submit to your husbands as to the Lord. [23] For the husband is the head of the wife as Christ is the head of the church, his body, of which he is the Savior. [24] Now as the church submits to Christ, so also wives should submit to their husbands in everything. [25] Husbands, love your wives, just as Christ loved the church and gave himself up for her [26] to make her holy, cleansing her by the washing with water through the word, [27] and to present her to himself as a radiant church, without stain or wrinkle or any other blemish, but holy and blameless. [28] In this same way, husbands ought to love their wives as their own bodies. He who loves his wife loves himself. [29] After all, no one ever hated his own body, but he feeds and cares for it, just as Christ does the church—[30] for we are members of

his body. [31] "For this reason a man will leave his father and mother and be united to his wife, and the two will become one flesh." [32] This is a profound mystery—but I am talking about Christ and the church. [33] However, each one of you also must love his wife as he loves himself, and the wife must respect her husband.

This passage of Scripture is probably the most often quoted on marriage in the Bible. Most of the time, people grab onto one word, "head" (in verse 23), and cluster on top of this one word like a whole baseball team on second base. From this unbalanced vantage, marriage concepts are developed that contradict not only Christ's teachings, but also Paul's as well.

For instance, it has become very popular for people to declare that love is the husband's role and submission is the wife's role—since wives are told to submit in Ephesians 5:22, and husbands are told to love in verse 25. But in order to come to this conclusion, the reader must ignore Paul's statement: "Be kind and compassionate to one another, forgiving each other, just as in Christ God forgave you. Be imitators of God, therefore, as dearly loved children and live a life of love, just as Christ loved us and gave himself up for us as a fragrant offering and sacrifice to God" (Ephesians 4:32–5:2). Notice that Paul's beginning words are generally directed to the body of Christ, of which Christian wives and husbands are a part. He tells *everyone* to be kind, compassionate, forgiving, to be imitators of God, and to live love in the same self-sacrificing way Christ did. Paul does not say that sacrificial love is a role. Instead, he encourages all Christians to live love and pour themselves out in selflessness for each other. This includes husbands *and* wives. Furthermore, it is in line with Christ's command to "love each other as I have loved you" (John 15:12).

In Ephesians 5:21, Paul makes another point: "Submit to one another out of reverence for Christ." Notice he does not say that submission is a role. He makes a thematic statement that goes hand-in-hand with his encouraging all believers to imitate Christ in self-sacrifice. You see, the essence of sacrificial love *is* submission. You cannot extract one from the other. Christ said, "Greater love has no one than this, that he lay down his life for his friends" (John 15:13). When a couple is in healthy submission to one another, they daily lay down their wishes, self, and lives for each other. Too often, submission is interpreted to mean obedience. This creates the father–husband, who views his wife more as a daughter he must manage than as his lifetime partner and lover. Mutual submission from a husband and wife has nothing to do with obedience and everything to do with selfless love. In Ephesians 6:1-3, Paul tells children to obey their parents. He never tells wives to obey their husbands or husbands to obey their wives.

In Ephesians 5:22-24, Paul addresses wives: "Wives, submit to your husbands as to the Lord. For the husband is the head of the wife as Christ is the head of the church, his body, of which he is the Savior. Now as the church submits to Christ, so also wives should submit to their husbands in everything." Then, he addresses husbands:

> Husbands, love your wives, just as Christ loved the church and gave himself up for her to make her holy, cleansing her by the washing with water through the word, and to present her to himself as a radiant church, without stain or wrinkle or any other blemish, but holy and blameless. In this same way, husbands ought to love their wives as their own bodies. He who loves his wife loves himself. After all, no one ever hated his own body, but he feeds and cares for it, just as Christ does the church—for we are members of his body (verses 25-30).

Understand that whatever is interpreted in the meaning of these scriptures, they cannot be assigned a meaning that violates Paul's other statements, or the teachings of Christ. One of Jesus' key teachings that cannot be ignored is the Golden Rule: "So in everything, do to others what you would have them do to you" (Matthew 7:12). Notice, Jesus said in *everything*. This includes the marital concepts we embrace and teach and the way we treat and think about our spouses. When a husband insists on his wife filling a role he would abhor filling himself, then his view is out of balance. Likewise, when a wife harbors attitudes against men she would not want directed to her, she is not exhibiting the heart of Christ.

Another of Jesus' key teachings involves the issues of servanthood. Repeatedly, He told His disciples not to elevate themselves, not even to call themselves "masters" or "leaders" (Matthew 23:10 KJV and NASB). When the disciples asked Jesus who was the greatest, He said, "Therefore, whoever humbles himself like this child is the greatest in the kingdom of heaven" (Matthew 18:4). Did Paul mean to set up or teach hierarchical marriage—that the husband is more of a father figure for the wife than a best friend and lover? Or was Paul teaching that as Christ came to serve, so husbands and wives are to serve each other? This second idea better aligns with numerous other scripture passages, including:

"The wife does not have authority over her own body, but the husband does; and likewise also the husband does not have authority over his own body, but the wife does" (1 Corinthians 7:4 NASB). In context, this refers to sexual issues. However, the ramifications support Paul's teaching on mutual submission.

"In the Lord, however, woman is not independent of man, nor is man independent of woman. For as woman came from man, so also man is born of woman. But everything comes from God"

(1 Corinthians 11:11-12). In context, this comes after instructions on the Jewish culture's order of worship. However, it also illustrates the healthy, interdependence of a man and woman within a Christian marriage.

"There is neither Jew nor Greek, slave nor free, male nor female, for you are all one in Christ Jesus" (Galatians 3:28). In context, this refers to the body of Christ, of which Christian wives and husbands are a part.

"If you have any encouragement from being united with Christ, if any comfort from his love, if any fellowship with the Spirit, if any tenderness and compassion, then make my joy complete by being like-minded, having the same love, being one in spirit and purpose. Do nothing out of selfish ambition or vain conceit, but in humility consider others better than yourselves. Each of you should look not only to your own interests, but also to the interests of others" (Philippians 2:1-4). In context, this refers to the body of Christ, of which Christian spouses are a part.

Since we believe Paul's writings are supportive of everything Christ taught, including servanthood, then we also believe that Paul had no intention of supporting hierarchal marriage. With this understanding, many noted scholars interpret "head" in Ephesians 5:23 to mean "fountainhead of life" or source.[2] Please notice that when Jesus told His disciples not to call themselves leaders, He did not tell them not to take or embrace positions of influence. What He told them was, in essence, don't use any position as a means to elevate the self and insist that people follow you. Husbands and wives who live this fully understand that they each influence the other while looking for ways to serve each other and make life better for the object of their love. These couples will never demean, demote, or limit each other.

They won't turn their back on the other and call, "Follow me!" over their shoulder. Instead, they'll say, "Come beside me, and we'll work together in unity and in the bond of Christ's love. I am not more important than you. We are important together."

True to his style, Paul says, " 'For this reason a man will leave his father and mother and be united to his wife, and the two will become one flesh.' This is a profound mystery—but I am talking about Christ and the church. However, each one of you also must love his wife as he loves himself, and the wife must respect her husband" (Ephesians 5:31-33). When a husband and wife become one, there is something highly mysterious and miraculous in the making. I see this as one partner mingling with the other so that they now have one mind, one set of arms, one face, and one heart. However, this level of oneness only occurs when both spouses commit to mutual love, mutual respect, and mutual submission.

Along with the Ephesians 5 passage, there are other scriptures where the man is referrred to as "head" of the woman. For instance, 1 Corinthians 11:3 states, "Now I want you to realize that the head of every man is Christ, and the head of the woman is man, and head of Christ is God." While it is important not to isolate a word or passage to the exclusion of others, it is just as important when searching Scripture to understand what the word or text would have meant to the audience to which it was written. The truth is, words sometimes change in meaning. And meanings are sometimes altered when words are translated from one language to another. The word "head" is no exception. In reference to 1 Corinthians 11:3, Lawrence O. Richards states,

> Despite efforts of some to impose hierarchical implications, Paul is clearly not using "head" in a superior/subordinate sense. Head, *kephale,* was not generally used in Greek literature in the sense of "chief" or "highest in rank." ...Paul's first-century readers would

have understood his metaphor to indicate "source of life" rather than "ruler" or "superior vs. inferior."... Paul wants to construct a framework for his [following] remarks. That framework is at once theological, historical, and relational. Christ is the source of man's life (John 1:4), Adam ("the man") is the source from which woman was formed, God Himself is the source from which the incarnate Christ came....From time to time we hear someone argue from this passage that men, the "head," are superior and women are inferior, so women must obey men. But how is Christ inferior to the Father, who is His "head"? From eternity, Father, Son, and Holy Spirit existed as one God, coequals although with different roles in carrying out the plan of salvation. We might much more logically argue for the *equality* of men and women from this verse than from woman's subordination. In fact, Paul does exactly this in stressing the interdependence of the sexes in 1 Corinthians 11:11-12....Paul's use of "head" here must not be taken to support a hierarchical view of male/female relations in home or church.[3]

Richards and numerous other contemporary Bible commentators are calling for viewing the husband and wife as equals. While this is a healthy and refreshing view of marriage, we must never forget that Christ continually calls us to be servants. Servant spouses willingly lay themselves down for each other. When both a husband and a wife commit to this level of amazing love, God's transforming power can and will create a miracle. This is the kind of breath-taking marriage Daniel and I have grown into. And Christ is ready to impart this type of heaven-on-earth marriage to you, as well.

> *Then Jesus said to his disciples,*
> *"If anyone would come after me,*
> *he must deny himself and*
> *take up his cross and follow me."*
> MATTHEW 16:24

What are some of the characteristics of marriages that don't fully practice mutual submission and servanthood?

- *Instead of a liftestyle of harmony, the spouses are trapped in an on-again, off-again "love affair."* The couple seems to deeply care for each other one day, week, or month, but can't stand each other the next. Wives in such unions are often heard saying something like, "I've never thought of divorcing him, although I have thought of murdering him."

- *The husband is a father–husband.* He views his wife as a person he must manage. Instead of viewing her as a spiritual and emotional adult, he believes he must lead her because she cannot spiritually function otherwise. This stunts the marriage because a father–husband will never truly respect his wife or believe that he can learn from her…or that God will communicate to her for their home and marriage. In healthy marriages, *both* partners encourage each other to read the Bible, pray, and attend church. They also share the responsibility of praying with and discipling the children. In these unions *both* spouses also spiritually learn from each other as they draw closer to Christ.

- *The wife views herself more as a daughter than a lover.* Women in these marriages aren't overtly sexual and probably seldom initiate sex. They actually see their husband as a father figure rather than a lover. Many of them spend their marriages fearing they will reap the disapproval of their father–husband if they speak up with spiritual insight.

∞ *Both spouses are likely to be disillusioned with each other.* The husband is exasperated with the wife—especially if she exhibits spiritual and emotional strengths he does not have. In turn, the wife feels as if she has to turn off who she really is in order to please her husband and, in some cases, the church. This brings perpetual disillusionment because the wife usually thinks that when they got married her husband would applaud her and empower her.

∞ *The wife is spiritually frustrated because she is encouraged to look to her husband instead of Christ for spiritual guidance.* Some wives have been taught that their husbands are their Jesus. Sometimes this is blatant; other times it's subtle. These wives believe their husbands are supposed to have superior spiritual wisdom. In truth, no man manifests this...neither does any woman, for that matter. When the husband doesn't show signs of superior spirituality on all fronts, the wife believes her husband is defective.

∞ *The husband lives a life of perpetual sexual frustration.* Women who believe their husbands are defective or father figures will not strive to fulfill them sexually. If a woman loses her respect for her husband, she will also lose her ability to amorously respond to his overtures.

∞ *The husband is "the commander"; his wife is his subordinate.* Oftentimes the husband despairs because his wife seems more bonded to their children than to him. This is the natural fallout of a wife being assigned within "the ranks" and placed "beneath" the husband in a child-like role.

It Was Night

by Ray N. Hawkins

I was afraid.
It was night.
You touched my hand.
I became stronger.
I was comforted.

I was lost,
so confused.
You called my name.
I ran to you.
I was found.

I was tired,
feverish.
You kissed my eyes.
I rested on you.
I had peace.

I was depressed;
life felt useless.
You prayed with me
I was unburdened.
I had hope.

I was alone.
You embraced me,
spoke words of love.
I was complete.
I was yours.[4]

From Daniel

Even though I don't have a degree in biblical studies or psychiatry, I do know how to read the Bible for myself. And I do know you can't take one word or section and run with it. You can come out with all sorts of weird stuff that way.

Sometimes, some of the unbalanced marriage concepts taught have made me angry, and I'm not even a woman. Not the last I checked, anyway! In those cases, I have felt as strong a need to defend my wife as if she were under physical attack because I felt as if she was under spiritual attack. There's nothing holy about encouraging husbands to view their wives as one rung beneath them. In doing so, we devalue every area of growth our wives have achieved.

Through the years, I have gleaned a great deal of wisdom from my wife. If it weren't for her, I would still be in the pit that I mentioned in chapter 3. I had enough sense to listen to what she was saying and to begin the journey to healing. If I had believed that I would always have all the answers spiritually, or that she was always supposed to follow me, I guess I would still be in that emotional pit. I think the smartest husbands tune into the counsel of their wives. Wives who feel that level of respect usually return it tenfold. And the wife in turn tunes into the counsel of her husband.

In this type of marriage, you get two spiritually and emotionally mature adults who are blending the best of who they are to become one whole. Then they put all they have into empowering each other in their weak areas. Man, I love my marriage!

Prayer Points for Romance

∽ Pray that the Lord will show you any spiritual attitudes toward your wife and your marriage that contradict the teachings of Christ.

∞ Ask Jesus to give you the wisdom to listen to your wife's wisdom.

∞ Beseech the Lord to break your mind free of any self-elevating thought patterns.

∞ Ask Christ to show you ways you can express selfless love to your wife.

∞ Pray that Jesus will deliver you from any fear that stops you from wholly releasing yourself to your wife.

Romantic Notions
by Richard L. Brunstetter

King Solomon made for himself the carriage;
he made it of wood from Lebanon. Its posts he made of silver,
its base of gold. Its seat was upholstered with purple,
its interior lovingly inlaid by the daughters of Jerusalem.

SONG OF SONGS 3:9-10

What I Did

Ever since I married my wife, Wanda, 41 years ago, she has told me she would like to take a limousine ride someday. Knowing that was a luxury we really couldn't afford, I didn't give the request much thought. When my daughter called me shortly before Wanda's sixtieth birthday and suggested we do something special for her mother, we both agreed it was time to get that limo ride for the pretty woman about to celebrate a very special day.

My Reason

I not only wanted to fulfill my wife's lifelong dream and make her feel special, but giving Wanda a ride in a limousine seemed like such a romantic thing to do. Our daughter Lorine made the arrangements with a limousine company near her home, and she kept me informed of the details as we planned.

How I Felt

I was excited because Lorine and I had planned something Wanda knew nothing about, but we were sure she would enjoy.

The Obstacles I Overcame

It wasn't easy to plan a surprise like this and not have my wife find out. Every time our daughter phoned to discuss the details, I was concerned that Wanda would overhear us talking and discover what we were up to. I had to be careful about what I said, and a couple times Lorine called on my cell phone when she knew I was away from the house.

My Wife's Response

Wanda knew about the plans we had to take her to dinner, but we threw her off when we stopped by our daughter's old house, which was up for sale. Lorine said she wanted us to see how it looked sitting empty. While we were touring the house, the limo pulled up. When we told Wanda to go to the door because someone was there for her, she seemed confused: "No one knows I'm here," she said. Wanda stepped onto the porch, and when she saw the limousine sitting in front of the house her mouth fell open. The driver held the car door for her and said, "You might be interested to know that this is the same limousine Julia Roberts rode in during the filming of the movie *Pretty Woman*."

I felt good about seeing my own "pretty woman" sitting in the exact spot a Hollywood star once occupied! I was delighted to know her dream had finally come true, and I'd played a part in it.

What I Wish I Had Done

My only regret is not having gotten a limousine ride for my wife sooner. Seeing how happy she was that night made me realize I need to do more romantic gestures and see that all of her dreams come true.

Budget Suggestions

A limousine ride might seem like a frivolous thing, but it was worth every penny. Since my daughter and I split the cost, it wasn't that expensive. If your budget is tight, try renting a nice vehicle from a car rental dealership. Dress up like a chauffeur yourself and act like you're a stranger trying to hit on her the whole time you're driving to the restaurant.[5]

What My Husband Does Right
by Lynette Sowell

- C.J. prays for me; often it's the last thing I hear before we fall asleep.

- He listens to my dreams and doesn't make fun of them.

- He shares the last piece of pie instead of keeping it all for himself.

- C.J. rubs my back even though he might be tired.

- He lets me pick the movie sometimes.

- He doesn't demand a before-bedtime romp when I'm especially tired; instead, we make the time another night and enjoy ourselves more.

- He apologizes when he is wrong.

- My husband keeps me laughing so I don't take myself too seriously.

- C.J. reminds me of God's promises when times are tough.

- He thinks I'm beautiful even when I don't look (or act) like it.[1]

Endearing Encounters

Until the day breaks and the shadows flee, turn, my lover,
and be like a gazelle or like a young stag on the rugged hills.
SONG OF SONGS 2:17

From Daniel

IF YOU WANT TO KNOW THE TRUTH, sometimes I feel romantically challenged. I know this book probably makes me sound like some Romeo who has everything together, but I just can't seem to view myself that way. When I start confessing this kind of stuff to Debra, she just rolls her eyes and tells me I'm way more romantic than I think I am. But that doesn't stop the way I *feel* about all this romance business. Anyway, if you're like me and feel somewhat romantically challenged, then this chapter is definitely for you. You'll find ideas from me as well as from some of our acquaintances. Some ideas are really basic, easy things to do, and some are what I think would appeal to the "advanced romantic." We hope you will find some inspirations that fit your budget and your lifestyle. Or maybe all you need is a few starter concepts to get your creative juices churning. From there, you can come up with your own endearing encounters.

We have designed a rating for each romantic notion. If an idea has one rose on it, then it will be quite easy and won't require a lot of planning or thought. A two-rose idea will require you to plot some. A three-rose idea might take several weeks to arrange.

Also, since each chapter has ended with an endearing encounter, by now you may be feeling as if you are swimming in new plans. That's understandable. I'd feel the same way. What we suggest is that you look at all the romantic notions in this book as a one- or two-year supply—depending on how busy you want to be. As you implement the ideas, check them off. Some you may even want to repeat!

1

A Would-Be Romantic Husband's Prayer

BY RAY N. HAWKINS

If you are a struggling romantic,
feel free to earnestly pray this exact prayer
or use this prayer as an example
and use your own words.

Lord,

I have a problem. Well, maybe it's not really a problem in the strictest sense, but it is for me. You know me, I'm not very articulate and I don't always express myself very well. I guess that's part of my timid nature, although the guys on the sports field would laugh at me being called timid. But I am. *You* know that.

Anyway, here's my problem. It's between me and my wife. Not so much her really, but me. You know I love her dearly, but I find it hard to show it. I'm not very adventurous or creative and things have, well, sort of become mundane in our relationship. We seem to have fallen into a rut...or is it a chasm? I don't know, but the old sparkle has become dull.

If I were a little bit more romantic, I know my wife would be thrilled. You understand—showing a bit more initiative in making her feel special, surprising her with something fancy and different. It makes me feel funny even talking about this with You 'cause I've never been that type of guy. But I'll do anything to bring back the sparkle to our relationship and break out of this rut.

Another thing, Lord, that worries me is if I give it a go, what will I do if she cries? What if she faints? Lord, what *would* I do if she faints?

In talking this over with You, I have a sense of excitement building 'cause I really do want to romance my wife. But to be honest, I'm not sure where to begin. Where can I lock into information that will give me holy and fun things to share with my wife?

Some people would probably think me stupid if they heard this prayer. I know You understand because You brought my wife and me together and want the best for us. Please turn my meditation into motivation. Put the fire into my spirit and the steel into my soul to overcome my timidity.

Lord, thanks for listening to me. I'll go now and ask her out to a dinner cruise on the river. This means I will miss watching my favorite sporting event, but so what! I can't cuddle a television. What I'd like to do afterward is take her up to that old special lookout of ours. There I'll tell her I love her and renew my vows to her. That should be the beginning of a whole new dimension to our love and loving. I'm getting excited by the thought!

One other thing…when I ask her, please, Lord, oh please, don't let her faint!

Amen.

Oh, What a Night!

Lord,

She didn't faint!

My wife did however scream and rush at me. The hug nearly took my breath away. I felt faint. She did cry. I admit, I even had a sniffle or two. What the neighbors thought if they heard the commotion, I hope I never know.

The cruise and dinner last night was wonderful. My wife looked stunning. She even said that I scrubbed up rather well myself. It was like the days just before and after our wedding. I felt like kicking myself for not doing this years ago.

What a night. So simple, so magical. When we were sitting on the deck chairs, it seemed as though the full moon sent its beams across the water to embrace us. Funny, isn't it, how things stay in the mind. She got the hiccups after dinner. Maybe I was the cause of it. My eyes couldn't, wouldn't, leave off looking at her. Her self-conscious, sparkling eyes looking up past half-lowered eyelids made my insides quiver.

Trying to steal a kiss or two between hiccups and other guests moving around was fun. We got the giggles. It's been a long time since we felt so young at heart. People did give us a quizzical look every now and then. They probably thought we were tipsy. Guess in a way we were. Not with alcohol. Love has been uncorked once more.

Song writing isn't part of my makeup, but I could have written her a love song last night. Wish I had, but I do feel self-conscious about such expressions of my feelings. Do You think she would mind if I gave it a go? Hope she doesn't think it silly or something like that.

Lord, You have given me a wonderful woman. To think that I nearly lost her in the mists of my self-preoccupation is rather frightening. Thanks for blowing the mists away. My wallet may be badly bruised, but my heart is full. Being together like last night beats anything money or acclaim can offer.

There is one thing that worries me, however.

My wife is now so excited by my newfound "romantic" openness that she's planning a surprise. She is on the internet now looking up sites for a weekend mountain retreat. It's for my birthday, she says. But I have to pay!

I think I'm going to cry—tears of excitement.

2

Wife and Mother of the Year

BY DANIEL W. SMITH

Charm is deceptive, and beauty is fleeting;
but a woman who fears the LORD is to be praised.
PROVERBS 31:30

What I Did

I decided to have a "Wife and Mother of the Year" dessert party for my wife. I bought a trophy and had it engraved: "Debra White Smith, Wife and Mother of the Year, 2004." I bought a cheesecake from the local deli. The kids and I aired up some balloons with helium and tied them to the chair backs in our formal dining room. We also bought some confetti bombs to pop when she walked into the room. Along with all that, we bought special cards for her and signed them.

My Reason

Debra gives so much to me and the kids, I wanted to do something very special for her.

How I Felt

Sly. I spent most of the day gathering the pieces of this little adventure. My wife has feelers out in all directions all the time, so getting anything by her is a miracle. I knew if I pulled this one off without her finding out, I'd have done something remarkable. I had to make the kids take a vow of secrecy, and I stayed tense most of the day because I was concerned they would slip.

The Obstacles I Overcame

The main obstacle was keeping the whole thing from Debra.

My Wife's Response

Amazingly, Debra had no clue we were scheming behind her back...until my son started whispering in my ear after dinner. Once he made a point of going into our formal dining room and coming out with a lame excuse for being in there, Debra discerned we were up to something. She hopped up from the dinner table and raced into the other room. We all followed and laughed. As soon as she entered the room, she saw the trophy, balloons, and cheesecake. The kids and I released the confetti pops. She "oohed" and "aahed" over the trophy and shone with pleasure.

What I Wish I Had Done

Originally, I wanted the trophy to just read "Wife of the Year," but since my kids were with me, they wanted to put "Mother" as well. I did that for them. After the party was over, I told Debra I would have preferred for the trophy to have just read "Wife of the Year" because my original intent was for this to be something just between me and her. As always, she was perfectly fine with everything the way it was.

Budget Suggestions

Since we already had the balloons and helium, I only had to purchase the trophy, the cheesecake, the confetti pops, and cards for a total of about $35. I was able to get Debra a really nice trophy for only $15 from a man who makes trophies in his home, so I saved some significant money there. Also, the man was able to make the trophy on the same day I ordered it. If you're on a tight budget, try baking a cake with a cake mix. If you've never cooked, the instructions on those boxes are very easy. Also, you can hand-make your cards or print them with your computer. You can buy a small container of helium from department stores in the party section or from party stores. Or you can just blow up balloons and tie the base of them to the tops of chairs. Since we were out of gift ribbon, we used sewing thread to tie the balloons to the chairs. If you just do the best you can with what you have, your wife will still be delighted with the thought.

3
Personal Slide Show

BY RONNIE JOHNSON

How is your beloved better than others, most beautiful of women? How is your beloved better than others?
SONG OF SONGS 5:9

What I Did

I created a personal slideshow for my wife's computer. I went through old photos to find pictures of just the two of us. I started with a picture from when we were first dating and ended with pictures from our twentieth anniversary. Using computer equipment I already had, I was able to scan the photos, create a slide show, and save it to a CD. I even selected one of our favorite songs to play in the background as the slide show ran.

My Reason

While on vacations or trips, I have cultivated the familiar habit of putting one arm around my wife and taking a picture with a camera held at arm's length in my other hand. I usually make sure there is something we want to remember in the background. Many pictures did not turn out well, but those that did found their way into the photo album. Putting these together created a visual record of 20 years of fun we've had together.

How I Felt

I felt anxious as I searched for at least one photo from every year we had been married. My wife is an organizer and usually has to help me find such things around the house. I also felt thankful for the years we have had together as I scanned the photos.

The Obstacles I Overcame

Finding the time to scan 40 photos was difficult. I attempted to do it when my wife was not home. Once she came home and asked me what I had been doing all afternoon. I just told her I had been wasting time at the computer. She wasn't surprised at that.

My Wife's Response

She knew I was working on scanning old photos to preserve on CDs. (That's what I told her to get her to help me find all the photo albums.) But I had not told her I was creating this CD for a Valentine's Day gift. She was surprised and appreciative. The very next day she took it to work to show to her co-workers.

What I Wish I Had Done

I wish I had been able to make a DVD that we could play on our DVD player and watch on TV. I may still do it!

Budget Suggestions

If you have the right computer equipment, this is very low cost. If you don't, then don't run out and buy a computer and scanner. Instead, find someone who has the equipment and know-how. If you have the computer equipment, you will also need basic slideshow software that can be purchased at any computer store. As a last resort, you can usually find someone who will scan and put your photos on a CD for a small fee. Your computer skill is not what your wife will appreciate. She'll appreciate the fact that you took the time to locate meaningful photos.[2]

4

Cowboy Firsts

BY JUDITH ROBINSON

Who is this coming up from the
desert leaning on her lover?
SONG OF SONGS 8:5

On our fifth anniversary, JB called me at work and asked me for a date. He wouldn't tell me where we were going, but dressed in the same type clothes he wore for our first date—blue jeans, cowboy shirt, and cowboy hat. He took me to the same restaurant we went to when we had our first date. We really laughed as we reminisced about our first date. I was starving the night we met, but I had been taught not to eat too much on the first date because it wasn't "polite" to spend too much of the guy's money so soon in a relationship. Consequently, I got a salad. He ordered enough food for both of us, but it was all for him! He kept offering me more to eat, but I kept refusing. What a dufus! I can assure you, I didn't just eat a salad on the night we recreated the date! Then, he took me to a $1 theater that just happened to be playing the same movie we saw on our first date! We were so romantically involved by the end of the movie, we went and "parked" for a while.[3]

5
Musical Message

BY DANIEL W. SMITH

My lover spoke and said to me,
"...See! The winter is past;
the rains are over and gone.
Flowers appear on the earth;
the season of singing has come,
the cooing of doves is heard in our land."
SONG OF SONGS 2:10-12

What I Did

I recorded a special cassette for my wife that featured several love songs that I felt spoke exactly how I feel. After presenting it to my wife, we've also enjoyed slow dancing to the music in our home or hotel room several times.

My Reason

I am musically inclined, so it's natural for me to express my love in this way. Also, I wanted to create something Debra could listen to when I wasn't around so she would be reminded of my continual love and admiration.

How I Felt

I must say this one really got my romantic juices flowing. I couldn't wait until she and I could listen to the tape together. Then, when I was able to hold her during the music, I really felt the power of my own love and hers.

The Obstacles I Overcame

It was a chore to get all the songs together. One I even recorded off the radio. I could have easily discarded the whole idea, but it was worth the effort.

My Wife's Response

Debra was elated with the songs! She even cried through some of them. She held me close while we danced.

What I Wish I Had Done

I wish I had added more songs. I stopped at five.

Budget Suggestions

This one was almost free. I already had some of the songs on cassettes and CD's. Remember, it's not the quality of the recording that's important—it's the sentiments expressed that are going to touch your wife's heart.

6

Picture Perfect

BY DEBRA WHITE SMITH

I am a wall, and my breasts are like towers.
Thus I have become in his eyes like
one bringing contentment.
SONG OF SONGS 8:10

One morning, the kids kept asking me if I was ready to do my makeup. After awhile, I started to get suspicious—especially when they began to giggle and whisper to Daniel. Daniel further increased my suspicion when he tried to get them to be quiet. I knew without doubt something was up, but I couldn't get any of them to tell me what. Finally, I gave up and went back to my morning routine. When I went into the bathroom, where I usually do my makeup, I was pleasantly surprised when I looked into the mirror. Daniel had used a red, dry-erase marker to write the words "Picture Perfect" and then drew a big square in the middle of the mirror—right where my face's reflection was. Delighted, I laughed out loud and called Daniel. He and the kids came into the bathroom and laughed with me. I kissed Daniel and hugged him and thanked him for the message. I loved the sentiment so much, I left it on the mirror. Months later, it's still there!

7

Quartet Romance

BY DANIEL W. SMITH

Eat, O friends, and drink; drink your fill, O lovers.
SONG OF SONGS 5:1

What I Did

I hired a barbershop quartet to sing to my wife in a restaurant on Valentine's Day. Since I wanted the time to be special, I arranged for my mother to keep our two kids. I also made reservations at our favorite Mexican food restaurant.

My Reason

Debra had been romancing me with great gusto and creativity. I wanted to do something that would surprise and delight her as much as she had me.

How I Felt

Mischievous and giddy. This was the most romantic thing I had ever pulled together, and I was anxious to see how she would react. Ironically, I came down with a stomach virus that day. By the time we were ready to go out to eat, I had turned a dull shade of gray-green. I felt so bad I didn't even have time to take the kids to my mother's. Debra knew I was ill and kept insisting that we not go to the restaurant. I insisted that we *should* go and wouldn't let her sway me.

The Obstacles I Overcame

My main obstacle was forcing myself not to throw up all over Debra and the kids in the restaurant! The other obstacle involved my reminding myself to keep the secret since I had booked the quartet several days before. Since Debra and I are best friends and tell each other everything, I caught myself a few times on the verge of just talking about the whole plan.

My Wife's Response

At first, she kept saying how impressed she was that I had made reservations. After all, we live in a tiny town, and this is a restaurant we frequent often. She thought it was very insightful and thoughtful that I even called ahead! When the quartet arrived, they presented Debra with a rose and began singing several songs. I don't believe I've ever seen Debra as radiant as she was that day. She would gaze at me and smile her adoration a while and then watch the quartet a while. The whole time she was blinking back tears. Just watching her so enjoy the special treat was probably one of the most fulfilling moments of my life.

What I Wish I Had Done

Early in our marriage, Debra was a bigger penny pincher than she is now. The first decade of our union, she would have discouraged me from doing something like this because she would have considered it an extravagance. A few times I thought of doing this sort of thing, but I had dismissed it because it is costly. After seeing the way Debra reacted, I now wish I had ignored her protests about over-spending during the first years of our marriage and done something like this a long time ago.

Budget Suggestions

This cost $100 for about 15 minutes worth of songs. We live in a small town, and I hired the quartet from the next largest town. In big cities, the price is probably higher. But if you're on a budget and like this idea, a local junior college or your church might have a quartet who would be willing to serenade your wife for much less.

8

One Hot Mama

BY BJ JENSEN

Come out, you daughters of Zion, and look at
King Solomon wearing the crown, the crown with
which his mother crowned him on the day of
his wedding, the day his heart rejoiced.
SONG OF SONGS 3:11

Teaching a chair exercise class for senior citizens that Valentine's Day a few years back was not exactly where I wanted to be that morning. My mind had raced ahead to the mall, where I had planned to buy that perfect romantic gift for my husband, Doug. I was sure the gift would reveal itself as I shopped. Doug and I had been married 10 years that year, so the gift had to be a special one.

Halfway through the class, a handsome man in a tuxedo walked through the back door. His ensemble was complete with a matching red bow tie and cummerbund. The handsome man was Doug! He had taken off work to hand-deliver a large bouquet of giant sunflowers. Smiling from ear to ear because of my look of astonishment, he handed me the beautiful bundle of sunshine and an obviously homemade Valentine card that read:

> Roses are red.
> Sunflowers are big.
> You're one hot mama
> I really dig.

With a hug and a kiss, Doug departed to the "oohs" and "aahs" of a room full of teary-eyed, grateful grannies who had just witnessed love in action.[4]

9

Pitching the Tent

BY DANIEL W. SMITH

Listen! My lover! Look! Here he comes,
leaping across the mountains, bounding over the hills.
My lover is like a gazelle or a young stag.
SONG OF SONGS 2:8

What I Did

Debra was participating in the Boy Scouts' "Mom and Me" weekend with my son. Normally, Debra and Brett work together to unload the van, arrange their campsite, and set up the tent. But this wasn't too long after Debra had surgery so I helped them pack, loaded the van, and followed them one hour to the Boy Scout camp to set up the tent. This was early Saturday morning. They were scheduled to come home early Sunday morning. So, Sunday morning before church I got up and drove back to the campground. Brett and I took down the tent and loaded the van. When we got home, Brett and I unloaded the van.

My Reason

I knew that if I didn't carry the physical burden for the "Mom and Me" weekend, Debra would not be able to go. Since my wife and son are elated to participate in this weekend, I couldn't let Debra's physical limitations hinder their participation. They really bond during this time together. Therefore, I decided to do everything in my power to make certain that Debra could go.

How I Felt

I was honored to be able to assist Debra. She gives selflessly to me and our children, and I'm always glad to be able to sacrifice for her.

The Obstacles I Overcame

I had to get up really early both mornings, around 6:00. Sunday was the hardest day. Since Sunday school starts at 9:45, we were rushed to get back home and get dressed in time. Also, this made for a long Sunday, and we were all tired that evening. I could have easily told Debra that she and Brett just shouldn't go this year because of her physical limitations, but I'm glad I didn't.

My Wife's Response

My wife fell all over herself to thank me and tell me how wonderful I am. I shamelessly absorbed her praise! Debra also said that numerous moms at the campground were highly impressed with my willingness to help her on this level.

What I Wish I Had Done

On the way home Sunday morning, we drove through a doughnut shop for some doughnuts and pigs-in-blankets. I wish I had gotten up in time to buy breakfast on the way to the camp. That way I could have offered Debra and Brett breakfast before we left the campground.

Budget Suggestions

This one just cost some gas, a few bucks for breakfast, and time. This is really one of those areas of sacrifice that transcends a dollar count. The main thing it cost me was some sleep!

10

Facing Fears for Each Other

BY JUDITH ROBINSON

My dove in the clefts of the rock,
in the hiding places on the mountainside,
show me your face, let me hear your voice;
for your voice is sweet, and your face is lovely.
SONG OF SONGS 2:14

When we went on vacation to Colorado Springs, my husband, JB, and I each had something we wanted to do that the other one didn't. He wanted to go down into a gold mine in a mountain. I'm claustrophobic! I wanted to ride the rapids down the Colorado River. He can't swim and is afraid of fast water! We both decided we would do what the other wanted and trust God to help us get past our fears. The Lord did and we did! We have pictures to prove it! I'm posing by a sign that says, "You are now 1000 feet underground." Like I needed to be reminded! We also have the picture of JB hanging on to the ropes on the side of a rubber raft as we swirled through the rapids. You can see the muscles standing out on his arms as he hangs on for his life.[5]

11

Pike's Peak
Bubble Bath

BY DEAN MILLS

The mandrakes send out their fragrance,
and at our door is every delicacy, both new and old,
that I have stored up for you, my lover.
SONG OF SONGS 7:13

What I Did

I prepared my wife a candle-lit bubble bath complete with Sparkling Grape Juice and romantic music playing in the background. I managed to get the bubbles to expand to three feet tall. Also, I included elements that would appeal to all five of her senses.

For the sense of taste, I had fortunately picked up a two-pack of Sparkling Grape Juice to help celebrate the New Year and still had an unopened bottle chilled in the refrigerator. For the sense of hearing, I played classical love songs on our piano. (If you aren't a pianist, browse the sampling kiosks at any department store and choose a CD she will enjoy.) I used candles to appeal to her sense of sight. For the senses of smell and touch, consider spending a little more on some nice fragrant bath bubbles or salts. Try to avoid the kids' Mr. Bubble, as your wife will definitely notice the difference. And remember, be generous with the bubbles. My wife loved the Pike's Peak effect!

My Reason

My wife had just returned from a hectic business conference and was in need of some relaxation.

How I Felt

I tried imagining how she must feel since I myself have returned many times after a busy time on the road. Realizing that she needed an opportunity to wind down for the evening, I figured a diversion from the normal routine was in order.

Obstacles I Overcame

I am typically not that spontaneous, so I was stretched to quickly put it all together without her really noticing what I was doing or that I was mysteriously absent from the rest of the house. While she was wrapping up things in the kitchen after dinner, I made brief visits in the kitchen while preparing things in the bathroom, in hopes she wouldn't suspect anything.

My Wife's Response

She was very surprised and quickly showed her appreciation. She wasted no time slipping into the tub and enjoying the Pike's Peak-like bubbles.

What I Wish I Had Done

I wish I had thought enough in advance to have a special dinner prepared when she arrived. I also wish I had arranged for her to have some chocolate-covered strawberries to enjoy once she finished with her bath.

Budget Suggestions

Sparkling Grape Juice is usually under $5, so that's pretty easy to cover. Candles can cost all amounts. Don't discount shopping at stores where everything is a dollar. It's amazing what you can find—even classical music CDs![6]

12

Sapphires on a Budget

BY JUDITH ROBINSON

O affflicted one, storm-tossed, and not comforted,
Behold, I will set your stones in antimony,
And your foundations I will lay in sapphires.
ISAIAH 54:11 NASB

JB's business had gone under in the massive depression of West Texas, like so many other businesses. We owed the bank more money than we thought we could possibly pay off. After much prayer, we decided to try. We met with the bank, made arrangements to reduce the interest and payments, and tightened our belts to come up with the money. It took us several years to pay off the debt, but we did. When the final payment was made, we rejoiced. Little did I know that my husband had been setting aside small amounts of money, sometimes only 50 cents, every payday. He went out the day after we paid off the debt and bought me a diamond and sapphire ring with the money he had been saving. He presented it to me on one of our "at home" dates. He said the ring represented how much he loved me for all the love and support I had given him over the years.[7]

13

A Romantic Interlude

BY DANIEL W. SMITH

*Like a lily among thorns is my
darling among the maidens.*
SONG OF SONGS 2:2

What I Did

Since Debra and I both have home-based businesses, we have two different phone lines. I was going to bed early one night while she stayed up working on one of her books. Since I'm on call around the clock for my business, I always place my cordless phone on the nightstand before going to bed. This particular night, after crawling into bed, I decided to call Debra on her line and sing "Have I Told You Lately that I Love You."

My Reason

I really love my wife and wanted to do something different to make her feel special.

How I Felt

As first, I felt a little vulnerable. I was worried Debra would think my idea was goofy. Then, I could only remeber the first part of the song and felt lost because I had to just stop. I was even more worried Debra would think the whole idea was a flop. After the way she reacted, I was elated beyond words.

The Obstacles I Overcame

The main thing I had to fight was my own hesitation. When I first thought of the idea, I dismissed it because I was afriad I would appear sappy.

My Wife's Response

Debra was silent the whole time I sang the song. I fully expected her to burst out laughing, but she didn't. Soon after I finished, I realized she was sniffling. The next thing I knew, she had left her office and hurried through the house to come crawl in bed with me. The kids saw her come into the bedroom and hurried in to pile into the bed with us, so all I got was a warm hug, a chaste kiss, and some serious cuddling. But the tears in Debra's eyes and the glow on her face was worth everything.

What I Wish I Had Done

I wish I could have remembered the whole song and that I had done this sort of thing years before.

Budget Suggestions

This one didn't cost me a thing. However, if you aren't a singer you can always get a CD and play it over the phone. Pretend you're a D.J., annoucing a special dedication from you to your wife. She'll love it…even if you aren't the one singing.

14
Keeping Romance Alive

BY RONNIE JOHNSON

Come away, my lover, and be like a gazelle
or like a young stag on the spice-laden mountains.
SONG OF SONGS 8:14

I will be the first to admit that I do not always follow these, but when I do, my wife appreciates it.

- Stop, look, and listen. I attempt to never get too busy to pay attention to my wife. Sometimes I consciously stop whatever I am doing and look at her. This alone will give me a lot of information concerning her mood, attitude, and sensitivity. Then I listen to what she says, how she says it, and the emotion behind it.

- Don't try to fix everything. Most of the time I find my wife just wants me to listen—not necessarily give answers.

- Frequently tell her that I love her. I know actions often speak louder than words, but she needs to hear the words also. Besides, I like saying them.

- Kiss her good morning, goodbye, hello, and good night every day. This is the bare minimum of kisses she gets each day.

- Go on at least one date per week. We need time for just the two of us.

- Give her an unexpected gift at least once a month.

- Help with housework.

- We do things we both enjoy, like going fishing.[8]

15

Tropical Paradise

BY RICHARD L. BRUNSTETTER

*My lover has gone down to his garden, to the beds of spices,
to browse in the gardens and to gather lilies. I am my lover's
and my lover is mine; he browses among the lilies.*
SONG OF SONGS 6:2-3

What I Did

For a long time my wife and I have wanted to go to Hawaii. Since we still haven't made it there, I planned an overnight stay at an inn that has numerous theme rooms. One of those rooms has a tropical theme. The bed was placed under a thatched roof, and there was a jetted tub for two built around rocks and ferns, with a cascading waterfall that doubled as a shower. Island scenes were painted on the walls, and seashells mixed with sand nestled inside a glass tabletop.

With our busy lives, we don't get much time away together, but we had a full 24 hours of soft music, island breezes, warm water, and a romantic interlude we'll never forget. While the hotel room certainly wasn't Hawaii, it did give us the enjoyment of being together in our own tropical paradise.

My Reason

I wanted to add a bit of romance to our busy lives, and at the same time get a hint of what Hawaii will be like if we ever make it there.

How I Felt

I enjoyed seeing the pleasure on Wanda's face when we stepped into the room and she saw all the tropical decorations. I also felt good about spending time alone with the woman I've been married to for more than 41 years.

The Obstacles I Overcame

The biggest obstacle I had was in finding time to make the trip. With Wanda's hectic writing schedule, and my busy life in full-time ministry and part-time painting, getting away is not always easy.

My Wife's Response

Wanda was pleased with the tropical-themed room, and she said she enjoyed her time alone with me as much I did with her. She commented, "This certainly isn't Hawaii, but I thank you for giving me a taste of what it's going to be like when we do finally get there."

What I Wish I Had Done

I wish I had started planning and saving for a trip to Hawaii many years ago, but I'm working on that now. Hopefully by our fiftieth anniversary, we'll be seeing the "real" tropical paradise of our dreams.

Budget Suggestions

One night at the inn cost a little over $200, so this was not an inexpensive romantic getaway. We also had the cost of our gasoline for the 12-hour round trip. However, this isn't something we do every day, and the price was worth the pleasure. If you can't afford a special room, think in terms of decorating your bedroom in a tropical or other fun theme.[9]

16

Two to Tango

BY JUDITH ROBINSON

Who is this that appears like the dawn,
fair as the moon, bright as the sun,
majestic as the stars in procession?
SONG OF SONGS 6:10

When we were first married, we had
custody of JB's two children, very little
money, and lots of stress. I love to dance,
and JB can't dance worth a flip. He surprised me by signing us up for dance lessons
at a dance studio so he could learn to dance.
This was pretty costly at the time, but it gave us a
weekly "date" where we laughed and had a great time. What a
hoot! It was the era of "disco," and I still crack up when I
remember how funny we looked trying to learn the disco moves.
It was a wonderful break from our routine and the stress of life!
We enjoyed it so much, we ended up taking lessons for country
dancing as well.[10]

17

Sneaky Fun

BY RICHARD L. BRUNSTETTER

*Come back, come back…
that [I] may gaze on you!*
SONG OF SONGS 6:13

What I Did

When our two children were young, we had to get a babysitter in order to go out or have romantic time alone at home. I came up with a way to surprise Wanda and work around the babysitter problem. Several times, when she would least expect it, I would kiss her goodbye and leave for work in the morning, not telling her I'd made arrangements with my boss to take the day off. After I knew the kids were at school, I would sneak home and surprise my wife, announcing that I was home for the day and we were all alone. On several occasions we took walks on the beach or through a nearby park. We went shopping and out to lunch a few times, or we just stayed home and spent the day romancing one another.

My Reason

My reason for sneaking home unannounced was to surprise my wife and give us some quality time together that was unplanned and unhurried.

How I Felt

Surprising Wanda felt good because she's not an easy person to fool. It also felt great to take a day off and spend the whole time with the woman I love.

The Obstacles I Overcame

The biggest obstacle was in getting the time off work, so I had to plan ahead several days. There was also the concern that Wanda might have made other plans for the day and wouldn't appreciate my surprise.

My Wife's Response

Wanda always acted surprised, even though I sneaked home on several occasions, and she might have come to expect the indulgence. Even if she had made other plans on those days, she rearranged her schedule so we could spend time together. She said she appreciated my sneaky act.

What I Wish I Had Done

My only regret is that I didn't plan for longer than just a day here and a day there to be with my wife. It would have been more fun and exciting if I'd had two or three days in a row to spend with her. If I'd been able to find someone to watch the kids, we might have gone out of town for some of those days.

Budget Suggestions

My sneaky dates were probably the least expensive of any we've ever had. I used vacation days whenever I took time off work, so I didn't lose any money by staying home. My whole goal in staying home was just to spend time with my wife. Whether we stayed home all day or took a walk and had a picnic lunch, the cost was minimal. A few times we went to lunch at a restaurant, but those were low-cost restaurants. If you have the budget, you can spend as much money as you like, but keep in mind that the whole idea is to *spend time* together.[11]

18

At-Home Spa

BY ANONYMOUS

How is your beloved better than others
most beautiful of women?
SONG OF SONGS 5:9

We can't afford a massage therapist or a day at the spa, but somedays I feel like I've been there! My dear husband will give me an hour-long massage with candles all around the room and soft music on the stereo. Then sometimes afterwards, he will either run me a bath with bubbles or paint my toenails.

19

Starry Canopy

BY RICHARD L. BRUNSTETTER

Until the day breaks and the shadows
flee, turn, my lover, and
be like a gazelle or like a young
stag on the rugged hills.
SONG OF SONGS 2:17

What I Did

Several years ago, when my wife and I were newly married, she wanted a canopy bed. Unable to afford that type of bed, I came up with an idea to give our room a romantic makeover. I first painted the ceiling dark blue. Next, I stuck glow-in-the-dark star-shaped stickers on the ceiling, in the pattern of the constellations. Then I hung pale blue curtains from rods nailed to the ceiling along three sides of our bed. The filmy curtains could either be tied back, for a canopy look, or left to drape on all sides, giving us privacy and the feel of royalty.

My Reason

I wanted to make our bedroom more romantic and create an enjoyable place for my wife and I to spend time alone together.

How I Felt

I had fun creating a room we could both enjoy and that had such a romantic feel.

The Obstacles I Overcame

Placing the stars on the ceiling identical to the constellations was tricky. However, when the lights were turned out at night, and we could lie in bed staring at our own starry sky, it was worth all the planning and work.

My Wife's Response

Wanda loved the way our mock-canopy bed made the room look. Even though we no longer live at that same house, we always have stars on the ceiling in our bedrooms. Often, when I turn out the lights, Wanda will squeeze my hand and say, "The stars are out, Honey. Isn't it great?"

What I Wish I Had Done

I would have liked to have given my wife a real canopy bed, but then if I had, we wouldn't have been able to see the ceiling full of stars, so I might have had to come up with some way to stick them to the canopy material.

Budget Suggestions

The most expensive part of our romantic bedroom was the cost of the curtains and rods. You can spend as much or as little on these items that you choose. Most discount department stores offer inexpensive curtains and curtain rods. The stick-on stars were less than $5, so turning our room into a starry canopy was a fairly reasonable venture.[12]

20
Surprise Date

BY SAMANTHA N. CUTSHALL

I held him and would not let him go.
SONG OF SONGS 3:4

I am newly married, and one thing my husband does that I adore is every Friday we go on a "date." He will take me to the movies or out to eat at a restaurant that we have never been to. We do something new and different every weekend. I always look forward to coming home after work on Friday and finding out what we are doing that evening. It makes me fall in love with him more and more.[13]

21

Flipping for Flowers!

BY C.J. SOWELL

I am a rose of Sharon,
a lily of the valleys.
SONG OF SONGS 2:1

What I Did

I had to pick up a few groceries at the store one Saturday night. My wife wasn't feeling very well, so I brought the kids with me. I saw a $5 bunch of fresh flowers and grabbed them for her. When we were dating, it was easier (and expected) to do these things. I had no special reason to buy her flowers, unless you count that she was sick. It wasn't our anniversary or Valentine's Day.

My Reason

"Just because," and also to help her feel better.

How I Felt

I knew she wasn't feeling well, so the chances of getting romantic that evening were small. But I was looking forward to cheering her up and helping her get better faster!

The Obstacles I Overcame

The main obstacle involved setting aside my own busy mind-set enough to see a perfect and easy opportunity to make my wife feel special.

My Wife's Response

She was really touched! Her warm appreciation made me want to repeat the act.

What I Wish I Had Done

I wish I had never gotten out of the habit of doing this "just because."

Budget Suggestions

Skip one of your lunches out during the week. Instead of going through the drive-through, go by your local large supermarket or "Super Center." You don't have to buy a 50-dollar florist's arrangement to touch your lady's heart.[14]

22

Roses and Coffee

BY JUDITH ROBINSON

*All night long on my bed I look
for the one my heart loves.*
SONG OF SONGS 3:1

When JB worked nights at a convenience store during a bout of looking for full-time employment, he used to sneak in about 6:00 in the morning and bring me a cup of coffee and a dozen of the famous Tyler, Texas roses about once a week. The store where he worked would have a delivery once a week, and he got first pick of the bunch. They were so beautiful! Even though we were broke at the time, it only cost $1, but it really made me feel special. To this day, he still brings me coffee in bed almost every day.[15]

23

Rapture Her with Roses

BY ERIC WIGGIN

The blossoming vines spread their fragrance.
SONG OF SONGS 2:13

Over 35 years of marriage I had occasionally bought flowers for my Dot,
always for special occasions, and they
were usually expensive. My practical
male soul resists paying for something so
fragile which perishes so quickly. Yet within
the heart of almost every woman lies a special
appreciation for beauty so deep some men fail to
fathom it. Denied beauty, a woman easily feels like life is a drudge.

One day I discovered a yellow rose tinged with orange in a
supermarket flower cooler. *Only $1.49 for a long-stem bloom,* I
thought. *She'd like that. Why not?*

Like it? Had Dot been milk chocolate, she'd have melted all over
the floor! That one rose began a practice, now a habit of over five
years, of buying Dottie roses every week. Sometimes it's a single
stem, three, six, a dozen or more—whatever I can get a deal on.
I'm sorry I hadn't begun this 35 years sooner.

So let this old Romeo speak from 41 years of marriage. Indulge
your wife's appreciation for beauty with flowers. Experiment until
you find exactly what gives her joy.

Wal-Mart and Sam's Club have the best deals on roses around
here, but be sure to examine the product:

∽ Pinch the blossoms to see if they are firm at the base.

∽ Never buy roses that are fully opened or that have begun to wilt.

∽ Look for the "sell by" date on the wrapper, and try to get those dated five to seven days ahead.

∽ Make friends with your store's flower manager and learn when the new shipments arrive.

∽ Consider not taking your wife with you when buying flowers. If your wife is like mine, she might be embarrassed at such splurging and try to talk you out of it.

The best deal I've seen: 18 lovely miniature roses in a blushing apricot hue for $3.88 at Wal-Mart. They're on the table as I write this.[16]

24
The Big Apple

BY STAN TOLER

Strengthen me with raisins, refresh me
with apples, for I am faint with love.
SONG OF SONGS 2:5

What I Did

Looking over our spring calendar, I noted that my wife had two days off, which makes for a long weekend. I called my travel agent and booked a getaway vacation to New York City.

My Reason

I travel a great deal with my seminars and try to include Linda in special travel rather than a work venue. Plus, we hadn't had time away since Christmas.

How I Felt

Knowing her love for Broadway and the Big Apple, I knew this would be a terrific weekend. I was so right. Everything fell into place, including timely air travel!

The Obstacles I Overcame

Trying to purchase Broadway tickets for the big shows is not easy in the spring. I was able to land orchestra seating for *Fiddler on the Roof*. It was a fantastic musical. We held hands like two teenagers!

My Wife's Response

She was like a kid in toyland. She loved eating breakfast at a local deli, dinner at Carmens, taking the ferry to Ellis Island and the Statue of Liberty. Also, we walked the busy streets and shopped at Macy's (mostly window shopping). We also strolled around Ground Zero and shed tears for the deceased.

Budget Suggestions

Search the internet for the cheaper weekend vacations. Also, plan to take some change for the cabs and subways![17]

25
Money-Saving
Travel Tips

BY ERIC WIGGIN

I belong to my lover, and his desire is for me.
Come, my lover, let us go to the countryside,
let us spend the night in the villages.
SONG OF SONGS 7:10-11

While cutting corners on some romantic gestures might not be the most glamorous consideration, if you're on a budget you may not have a choice. Even if your budget isn't tight, it's always good to look for choice deals on hotel rooms, auto rentals, and plane tickets. Some of the following hints are tested means to saving some big bucks.

    ∾ *Hotel Rooms.* If your plans are flexible, pick up those pamphlets available at McDonald's, Shoneys, and at a lot of gas stations, and use their coupons. Look for AAA/American Automobile Association-rated motels on off-the-path roads. The Interstate highways were mostly built in the 1960s. Many of them parallel older U.S. highways, which often had fine motels built in the 1940s and 1950s. Many are still in business and have clean rooms for under $40. My son recently went through Priceline.com to bid on a room in downtown Chicago. He wound up getting a $225 room at a four-star hotel for $55. The hotel was an old one, built in the 1930s, but the place had been refurbished and was posh. These deals are available midweek—especially off-season. If you're on a budget, never try to book in a resort area during peak season. We've found great deals and empty beaches in the off-season at Myrtle Beach, SC, and Galveston, TX. At Myrtle Beach, we enjoyed balmy weather and long, palm-lined beaches, although the weather was a little cool for swimming. In Galveston, we found an oceanside hotel in December for $44. Restaurants were nearly empty, and waiters were hanging over us like flies. While Motel 6 isn't glamorous, you can stay there for around $40 a night. Also remember that most Super 8 Motels offer rooms in the $50-$60 range and provide a continental breakfast.

∞ *Plane Tickets.* Ticket purchases made after 1:00 A.M. sometimes get a better price because that's when airlines dump their cheap tickets. My daughter-in-law flew round-trip Dallas to Boston for $75. I got my wife a round trip-ticket from Portland, Maine, to Grand Rapids, Michigan, for $98. I think we both used Travelocity.com. My brother and wife flew round-trip from Milwaukee to London, England, for $200 apiece! Some of these flights require three-weeks notice, but they're worth it.

∞ *Auto Rentals.* We often travel in rented cars for under $30 a day by using specials. Rent midweek—that's when auto rental lots are full and companies are trying to push them out. You get the lowest prices, even though you may be renting for months away. Also Sam's Club and AARP memberships will earn 10 to 15 percent off several auto rental agencies. Or, if you know you're taking a trip, start watching for specials. When you see a good special, rent in advance. You can always change the date on the reservation if you need to make last minute change

What My Husband Does Right

by Alicia Johnson

- I enjoyed the way Ronnie showed me he was interested in me before we were dating. He left a single silk yellow rose on the windshield of my car without a note of who it was from. Later he came forward and confessed.

- Ronnie took me on a special lunch picnic at Jim Hogg State Park. He had visited the park the day before and hid things. We used a "Treasure Map" to find them. Some of the things were gifts for me.

- He sends me flowers at work for no reason.

- He also delivers flowers to me at work unexpectedly.

- He surprised me with an outdoor swing he built himself.

- Ronnie and I enjoy soaking in the hot tub at night under the stars!

- On our anniversary trip to Hawaii, he left homemade notes among my clothing in my luggage.

- Before he left on a week-long trip, he changed the start-up message on the computer by recording, in his voice, "Alicia, you can turn me on anytime" when I turned on the computer and "I love you" when I turned it off.

- Ronnie created a CD with "our song" showing different pictures of us throughout the years and another with our wedding pictures with a love song.

- He took time from his busy day to take me to lunch on Valentine's Day.[1]

Rekindling the Flames

Behold, the former things have come to pass,
now I declare new things; before they spring forth I
proclaim them to you. Sing to the LORD a new song,
sing His praise from the end of the earth!
ISAIAH 42:9-10 NASB

I HOPE YOU HAVE BEGUN TO IMPLEMENT some of the exciting concepts you have already encountered! As we have read through this project, Daniel and I have been drawn even closer together as we reflect upon our ever-deepening love for each other. This chapter contains two weeks of devotionals that you can use during your prayer time. Feel free to ask your wife to share this experience with you. Most godly women are thrilled to share prayer and Bible reading with their husbands. These devotionals work as a great dialogue tool as well. Discuss the issues with God, but also discuss them with each other. As in the previous chapter, we have purposefully included some pieces from other people to help broaden the perspective and enrich your reading experience. We hope the following pages will serve to invigorate your journey of romancing your wife.

1

The Flower

O daughters of Jerusalem, I charge you—
if you find my lover, what will you tell him?
Tell him I am faint with love.
SONG OF SONGS 5:8

Passage: Song of Songs 5

While attending a marriage seminar on communication, Tom and his wife, Linda, listened to the instructor declare: "It is essential that husbands and wives know the things that are important to each other."

He addressed the men: "For instance, gentlemen, can you name your wife's favorite flower?"

Tom leaned over, touched his wife's arm gently and whispered, "Pillsbury All Purpose, isn't it?"

The rest of the story is not pleasant![2]

How well do you know your wife and what is going on in her mind? Have you taken the time to really get to know her? If not, you may make mistakes similar to the one above.

When a man takes the time to connect with his wife—to get into her world and her thoughts—she will respond in a way that will astound you.

How long has it been since your wife was "faint with love"? Believe it or not, you have the power to make her feel that way— even if you've been married for decades! But it takes time, commitment, and a willingness to lavish your attention upon the woman you promised to cherish.

Dear heavenly Father, show me where I need to improve as a husband. Give me the strength and courage to end any activities that are wasting my time so that I can invest that time in our marriage relationship. Please, Lord, show me how I can make my wife feel like royalty!

2

Looking for Better Opportunities

by Chuck Noon

*Live happily with the woman you love through the
fleeting days of life, for the wife God gives you is your
best reward down here for all your earthly toil.*
Ecclesiastes 9:9 tlb

Passage: Ecclesiastes 9:7-10

For men, it's human nature to identify ourselves with job and career. Our self-esteem is based upon what we do, on our job title. The world daily reinforces this with emphasis on self, status, and the acquisition of personal net worth. In this narcissistic world, a wife becomes a possession, an extension of the self. The "trophy wife" is an example of this.

God's model is the opposite. God emphasizes treasure in heaven and dedication to our wives here on earth. "Husbands love your wives, just as Christ loved the church and gave himself up for her" (Ephesians 5:25).

My wife, Marita Littauer, has followed me in several moves as I pursued success. While I always had a job, I couldn't quite get ahead. Believing that better opportunities awaited me in Colorado, I became licensed there, took a job, and rented a small apartment.

Marita made the best of it, but it was very hard on her. She couldn't easily move. God has blessed her ministry in Albuquerque with great employees. She has wonderful friends and is very happy there. Seeking to keep the marriage alive, Marita drove back and forth between Albuquerque and Colorado Springs—

five-and-a-half-hours—almost every weekend. She was stressed and exhausted and had three automobile accidents during that six months.

One evening while I was out walking my dog, Harley, in the snow, wishing he would hurry up and do his thing, God spoke to me. Now, God has only spoken to me in a clear, audible voice three or four times in my life. So when He does, I listen. God told me, "Go home and take care of your wife." This was not what I wanted to hear, as God's direction seldom is. I thought that if I was going to do this, I really ought to be in the same state. I obeyed and moved back to New Mexico. I took a job that I considered to be way beneath my abilities and education. For a year-and-a-half, I worked in this humble position. During that time, I read the Bible cover-to-cover, and God went to work where He couldn't before. I didn't look for a better job, I waited for God to *select one for me.*

Once I put my wife first, not my career or my search for success, I was offered a job in my field that was impressive and paid more than I had ever made. Since that time, I have been offered many other positions and have my pick of opportunities. When I was seeking success and my own interests, success eluded me. When I was willing to put God in the driver's seat, and do what was best for my marriage (basically love Marita extravagantly), I found the success I worked so hard to find.

While God's way doesn't seem to make sense to the world, it is the best.

> *Lord, help me make Your priorities my priorities. I desire Your best for my marriage, my job, my life, and my wife.*[3]

3

Thank You, Lord

Sing and make music in your heart to the Lord,
always giving thanks to God the Father for everything,
in the name of our Lord Jesus Christ.
EPHESIANS 5:19-20

Passage: Ephesians 5:1-21

How often do you thank God for your wife? Why not take the time to make a list of the things you are thankful for in her? Then ponder each point and breathe a prayer of thanksgiving for the wonderful woman God has placed in your life. Better yet, after you make the list, sit down with your wife, read your list to her, and allow her to hear your prayer of thanksgiving. If need be, use the following prayer from R.N. Hawkins as your model.

> *Lord, it's 40 years coming up since my wife and I com-*
> *mitted ourselves to each other. It seems like it was simply*
> *earlier this morning. The time since then has been a dis-*
> *covery of the truth of 1 Corinthians 13. Truly, faith, hope,*
> *love abide to permeate all facets of our togetherness,*
> *family, and ministry. The reason for this prayer is simply*
> *to say "thanks" for Your gift to me of my wife. I know You*
> *won't mind if I try to say how I feel in picturesque ways.*
> *I just want to be a little bit more daring than the usual*
> *bland way I talk.*
>
> *My wife has been like the dawn that kisses the dark of*
> *night away. Many a time she has been like that in the*
> *midst of the darkness of life's pressures. I am grateful to*
> *You for those occasions when she has been Your refreshing*
> *breeze to my wilting endeavors. How often she has*

refreshed me over these years. You know she isn't perfect, wonderful as she is. As a volcano has its awesome beauty and danger zones, so too my wife. Fortunately, by Your grace and her self-awareness, she has controlled this tendency. I praise Your name that she has the spiritual capacity and courage to recognize and deal with this part of her nature. Thank You for your healing of any "lava" scalds and the power of forgiveness when it has happened.

Strange as it may sound, my wife is like a hot shower after a weary day. A shower seems to revive the tired soul, reinvigorate aching muscles, and cause lips to sing. The woman You have given me is like that with her cascading caresses and tenderness. Sure there have been times when I've seen storm clouds in her eyes. Often, mostly, these are justified. My rashness, brashness, harshness have been checked by that look. Still, Lord, I rejoice that through those clouds in her eyes I've beheld the rainbow of grace.

I kneel before You in celebration of that day when You joined us together in "one flesh." Since then You have shaped us, honed us, colored and flavored us for Your purposes. You have made us a team and made each complement the other for Your honor. Thanks. We know not how long we have in this world, but this we know: You will hold us together in Your hand and heart. For the hope that takes us beyond this realm, I praise You and that there, we will, together, see You face-to-face.[4]

4
The Shoe Box

*In your anger do not sin. Do not let the sun go down while you
are still angry, and do not give the devil a foothold....
Do not let any unwholesome talk come out of your mouths,
but only what is helpful for building others up according
to their needs, that it may benefit those who listen.*
Ephesians 4:26-27,29

Passage: Ephesians 4

There was once a man and woman who had been married for more than 60 years. They had shared everything. They had talked about everything. They kept no secrets from each other except that the old woman had a shoe box in the top of her closet that she cautioned her husband never to open or ask her about.

For all of these years, he had never thought about the box, but one day the little old woman got very sick and the doctor said she would not recover. In trying to sort out their affairs, the little old man took down the shoe box and took it to his wife's bedside. She agreed that it was time that he should know what was in the box. When he opened it, he found two crocheted doilies and a stack of money totaling $25,000. He asked her about the contents.

"When we were to be married," she said, "my grandmother told me the secret of a happy marriage was to never argue. She told me that if I ever got angry with you, I should just keep quiet and crochet a doily."

The little old man was so moved, he had to fight back tears. Only two precious doilies were in the box. She had only been angry with him two times in all those years of living and loving. He almost burst with happiness.

"Honey," he said, "that explains the doilies, but what about all of this money? Where did it come from?"

"Oh," she said, "that's the money I made from selling the doilies."[5]

What is your marriage like? Is there true harmony and peace? Or is there peace only because one of you is covering issues? Maybe there isn't peace or harmony at all. Perhaps you are in a cycle of conflict, living from one explosion of anger to another. There are some people who would have $125,000 in the doily box at the end of their marriages.

You know, your life doesn't have to be like that. You can break sinful behavioral patterns. Repeated conflict, anger, and a lifestyle of arguing over turf has never been and never will be God's prescription for a happy marriage. Domestic civil war is the fallout of sin-based concepts and hearts that aren't centered upon Christ. If one of you will commit to change, your marriage can be improved. If *both* of you will commit to change, your marriage can be revolutionized!

> *Dear Lord, forgive me for the times I've lived wrath rather than righteousness. Give me a glimpse of the peace that can exist in my marriage. Deliver me and my wife from the chains of any generational anger that is destroying our home's happiness.*

5

A One-Couple Christmas Trip

*The shepherds returned, glorifying and praising God
for all the things they had heard and seen,
which were just as they had been told.*

LUKE 2:20

Passage: Luke 2:1-20

A couple of years ago, I began to feel like I wanted to go away somewhere for Christmas. We have family nearby and enjoy a strong family tradition of getting together during all holidays. But that year, I really just felt a restlessness that insisted we do something different for Christmas.

Eventually, I couldn't ignore the urge to "fly." I knew I had to tell my husband. I said, "Daniel, what would you think about our going away somewhere this year for Christmas?"

He said, "You know, I've been thinking I'd like to do the exact same thing. Christmas is always so hectic, and I'm starting to think I'd like to go somewhere where we can enjoy a quiet time with just the four of us."

"That's exactly the way I feel," I responded. "What would you think about going to Jefferson?" This is a small, east Texas town about an hour from where we live. The city is quaint and not highly populated, but it is a large tourist attraction because of its vast array of old Southern mansions and antique shops.

"Hey, that sounds great!" he agreed.

So that year we allowed our children to unwrap their gifts early, and then we left town. For around a hundred dollars, we rented a little cabin in the woods. Christmas Eve night, we built a fire in the fireplace, played board games with our children, and watched *It's a Wonderful Life*. Christmas Day we wound up eating dinner at an exquisite Victorian mansion turned bed and breakfast. We made new acquaintances and enjoyed a delightful meal that none of us had to exhaust ourselves over. After eating, we took the kids to see a movie.

This Christmas excursion is turning into one of our fondest holiday memories. We got away from the norm and enjoyed a unity of spirit that no money can buy. Like the shepherds, we returned home "glorifying and praising God" because we were able to ponder the *true* meaning of Christmas without the rush.

When couples truly become one, an unfathomable peace descends upon them. My husband and I were *both* thinking we wanted to get away that Christmas, and we hadn't even consulted each other. We *both* had a need for simplicity and solitude that year. Because we are one, even our needs often reflect each other. When it came time to decide where we would go, where we would stay, and what we would do, there was no argument or dissension. There was just a joint desire to be together. The rest was mere details.

> *Jesus, Son of God, help me and my wife become one.*
> *Show me where I am battling for turf in my marriage,*
> *and give me the grace to change. Amen.*

6

A Near Miss

*Give ear to my words, O L*ORD*, consider my sighing.*
Listen to my cry for help, my King and my God,
*for to you I pray.…For surely, O L*ORD*, you bless the righteous;*
you surround them with your favor as with a shield.

PSALM 5:1-2,12

Passage: Psalm 5

One Sunday afternoon when our children were small, Daniel was out in our minivan, taking my mother to her home in the next town. A storm had rolled in, and the heavens were pelting the earth with "showers of blessings." I had lain down with the kids for a nap but couldn't sleep, which is unusual for a Sunday afternoon. Since I had yet to have my devotion that day, I felt the need to spend some time in prayer and Bible reading.

I sat down in our recliner in the den, opened my Bible, and began to read. My attention was drawn to the window and the heavy rainfall. A strong thought occurred to me that I could not shake: "Daniel could get killed in this weather." Immediately I began to beseech the Lord for my husband's protection. After a season of prayer, the rain diminished to a drizzle, and I sensed that the burden for my husband had lifted from my soul. I finished my Bible reading and began to busy myself around the house.

A while later, I was near our bedroom when my husband entered the room. He had a desperate look on his face. He was wet and worried. "Debra," he said, "I have had a *terrible* wreck." He explained that he got home only because a kind, older couple had offered him a ride. He had to leave the van on the side of the road in the ditch where it had slid. He then detailed exactly what happened.

"I was driving within the speed limit when the van started hydroplaning. Even though I didn't panic or try to over-correct the steering, the van immediately went into a spin. I twirled around and around, going across the other lane. Thankfully, nobody else was coming, or I'd be *dead!* I saw the ditch coming, and the next thing I knew, I crashed into it. I think the van is totaled!"

I stood with my mouth open. "Are you okay?" I asked and offered a tight hug.

"Yes, I'm fine. I don't have a scratch on me, but we can just kiss that van goodbye!"

"I don't give a hoot about that van. I'm just glad *you're* okay!" I said.

Clearly shaken, Daniel continued, "You know what, Debra? I have this strong feeling I just can't shake. It was like this huge hand scooped me to safety in that ditch. I wound up sliding in backward. So, the *back* of the van is demolished. If I had gone in nose first, it might have crushed me, and I think the back weight would have shoved the van into a roll." He rubbed his ashen face. "During the whole thing, all I could think was, 'This is it! I've lived my last day!' But then I just gracefully slid into that ditch backward. It was amazing and scary!"

My eyes wide, I said, "You're never going to believe this, but I was having my devotions and a strong thought came to me that you could get killed in this weather. I immediately began to pray for you! I wouldn't be surprised if I was praying for you at the same time you were spinning. Really, the impression was so strong that none of this story surprises me in the least!"

When a couple becomes one, God can use that very connectedness as a means to communicate the urgent need for prayer. This driving incident happened about five years ago. At that point in our marriage, we were just beginning the journey to true oneness. When I began to feel concerned about the weather and about my husband's being out, God placed a strong thought in my mind that required urgent intercession. Looking back, it is extremely strange that I was unable to sleep that Sunday afternoon. Usually, I fall into a coma every Sunday after lunch. I believe that my inability to sleep was my spirit being in tune with God's spirit and with my husband to the point that I was drawn to prayer.

How close are you and your wife to being a one-couple? Have you even started the journey? One day, your life or hers might depend on your ability to sense danger, hear the voice of God, and intercede on each other's behalf.

> *Dear God, reveal this great mystery to me! I'm not even sure how to fully become one with my spouse. Please show me if there is anything I'm doing to stop this amazing kind of marriage from happening in my own union.*

7

An Incredible Woman

He who finds a wife finds what is good and
receives favor from the LORD.
PROVERBS 18:22

Passage: Proverbs 18

My friend Kim recently discovered a wreck on the side of the road. She was one of the first people on the scene. A vehicle was turned upside down, and a woman was trapped inside. Kim was the only person with a cell phone. First, she called 911. Then, she started talking to the woman, who was terrified and on the brink of unconsciousness. Refusing to be a silent onlooker, Kim decided the woman needed someone close to support her, to pray with her, and to keep her talking to help prevent her from losing consciousness. So Kim managed to crawl into the vehicle with the lady. While they waited on the ambulance and authorities, Kim encouraged the woman and prayed with her. Once the ambulance arrived, so did the jaws of life, a big piece of machinery that cuts open a vehicle to free a trapped passenger. When the lady was freed from the vehicle, Kim assisted the paramedics any way she could. Only after they whisked the patient to the hospital, did Kim go home. However, she called the victim—who was also a Christian—to check on her during her hospital stay.

What Kim did was brave, honorable, and spiritual. She is truly a woman of God who has a deep and powerful relationship with her holy Creator. She not only blesses those she encounters, but she also blesses her husband with her mighty walk with Jesus.

What about your wife? What strengths make her incredible? Maybe she has the most productive garden you have ever seen. Perhaps she can cook better than anyone you've met. She might be a gifted Bible teacher. Her education could be extensive. Ponder the times she has shone with God-given courage and strength.

Wise husbands celebrate their wives' strengths. Smart wives don't expect their husbands to be something they'll never be. Together, these spouses are free to be who they are. While they recognize each other's positive capacities, they also acknowledge their individual weaknesses. From there, they commit to building each other up in those areas that are lacking.

This kind of marriage turns into a celebration of unity.

> *Lord, show me my wife's strengths. Give me the character not to scorn her weaknesses or try to press her into a mold she doesn't fit. Thank You for the incredible woman You have given me! Never let me forget that You have given her to me as a treasure to be cherished.*

8
Romance in Crisis

BY RONNIE JOHNSON

[Job's] wife said to him,
"Are you still holding on to your integrity?
Curse God and die!"
JOB 2:9

Passage: Job 1–2

What will you say to your spouse during a shared crisis? What will happen to your relationship when faced with a major stress? Marriages often break up in the wake of crisis situations such as an unforeseeable financial blow, the death of a child, or a chronic illness.

Is your marriage strong enough to survive even one of these situations? All of the above happened to a married couple in the book of Job, the first place many turn in the Bible for advice on suffering. Although there is only a brief exchange recorded between Job and his wife, you can follow their example for strengthening your marriage when faced with a crisis.

Even though Job's wife gave the disturbing counsel to "curse God and die," she was exemplifying a helpful principle: Communicate with your spouse! She shared deep feelings of anger and hurt. Her anger at God is not surprising when we remember all that she had lost. Apparently she was not happy with the way Job was holding on to his faith. Satan's attacks on her husband had worked on her. Job's response does not appear to be too kind at first glance. He told her she was talking "like a foolish woman" (Job 2:10). But next, he asked her a question that revealed the reason he held on to his faith: "Shall we accept good from God, and not trouble?" (Job 2:10). We know what Job said to her, but not how he said it. He may have made this reply with a kind, understanding attitude. It may have been just what she needed to hear.

Their deep level of communication is what we need to emulate. They were communicating on an emotional level. Sharing your feelings with your spouse can be scary. What if she doesn't react with the same level of emotion as you? What if she calls you foolish or ungodly? Accepting the feelings your wife shares can be equally frightening. You have to listen and not judge. You need to remember that your spouse might not react the same way as you.

If your marriage is going to be strengthened through a crisis, you must communicate. Your relationship is worth the risk. Talk it out. Suppressed feelings and losing focus on your commitment to each other may result in depression, isolation, hopelessness, blame, or resentment.

My wife and I learned by experience how our commitment to each other helped us successfully endure a crisis situation. While in graduate school, I was diagnosed with an illness that required three months of bed rest. We faced this crisis together, and our marriage was strengthened, but not before working through some emotional turmoil.

Unlike Job's wife, we did not communicate our deepest fears and emotions. I did not tell my wife that I was feeling inadequate and ashamed. I was also feeling guilty because my illness was stress-related. I simply had not taken care of myself while under the stress of graduate school. We had moved 200 miles from home and had both worked minimum-wage jobs to cover rent, tuition, and other expenses. Now I couldn't complete my degree or even work to pay the mounting bills for specialists, medical tests, and prescription drugs.

I also worried how I would ever be able to pay my wife back for everything she was doing for me. Of course, getting "paid back" was not on my wife's mind at all. I learned later that she kept much of her fear and distress hidden from me because she did not want to put any more stress on me than I already had. She busied herself at work to pay the bills, even while she worried about leaving me home alone. Because of our commitment to each other, we were constantly thinking about each other and not about ourselves. Anger on either of our parts would have been understandable and natural. I had been sure God wanted me in that place, at that time, yet it was all taken away. My wife's hopes and dreams had also faltered.

A couple of weeks of this emotional turmoil would be enough to put a strain on the best of marriages. Those three months would have been unbearable had we not had a strong commitment to each other and a common source of strength—our faith in God. Even though we failed in our communication efforts, our commitment to each other never wavered. We learned to accept whatever God had in store for us. I am glad to say that, as with Job and his wife, God has given greater blessings since that crisis passed.

> *Father, I know our marriage cannot float along crisis-free for our whole lives. Help me to prepare now for any crisis that might descend upon us. Oh, Lord, don't let me be hit by surprise and then not be able to maintain my relationship with my wife. No matter what happens now or in the future, I want to have the spiritual strength so that my wife and I can keep our family together. Please grow me into the spiritually mature man You want me to be.*[6]

9

Being Quick to Listen

BY PHILIP ATTEBERY

My dear brothers, take note of this: Everyone should be
quick to listen, slow to speak and slow to become angry,
for man's anger does not bring about the
righteous life that God desires.
JAMES 1:19-20

Passage: James 1

Most of us are aware of how important it is for a husband to communicate well with his wife. I often find myself to be quick-tempered and quick to speak rather than making it a priority to listen. I also find myself planning what I am going to say next rather than making a genuine effort to listen and understand what concerns my wife. I am certain that such reactions come from my own attitude of self-centeredness.

Philippians 2:3-4 says, "Do nothing out of selfish ambition or vain conceit, but in humility consider others better than yourselves. Each of you should look not only to your own interests, but also to the interests of others." If I can have such an attitude toward my wife, what a difference it will make in our efforts to communicate!

James 1:19 states, "My dear brothers, take note of this: Everyone should be quick to listen…." Being quick to listen must include at least two elements. First, I must be in a literal position to hear the words my wife says. Yelling across the house or over the volume of a television program hinder good listening. Second, I must try to understand the meaning or intent of her words. Consider these words that are stamped on a plaque I have: "I know you believe you understand what you think I said. But I'm not sure you realize that what you heard is not what I meant!" By simply repeating or rephrasing what you believe she has said helps her see that you have begun to understand her concerns.

James 1:19 continues with being "slow to speak." You may have a quick wit and be able to out debate your wife, but remember to consider her interests above your own. Pray daily for the ability to think before you speak and for the willingness to admit when you're wrong. Proverbs 10:19 says, "When there are many words, transgression is unavoidable, but he who restrains his lips is wise" (NASB). Wisdom involves listening first and speaking few words. Transgression is intentional wrongdoing. Isn't it true that the words exchanged during verbal arguments are often intended to do harm? Put the self-centeredness aside and clear the way for effective communication with your spouse.

James 1:19-20 continues, "and slow to become angry, for man's anger does not bring about the righteous life that God desires." Obviously, there are many ways to handle anger. I may be slow to speak but actually allow anger to build up inside until it explodes. Proverbs 29:11 says, "A fool gives full vent to his anger, but a wise man keeps himself under control." Even Jesus got angry—but He lived according to Psalm 4:4: "In your anger do not sin." Often when a person is upset, he does not slow down and try to understand the real issues and concerns of the situation that has provoked his anger. The result is often an attack on the other person. Jesus warned in Matthew 5:22 against anger that resulted in name-calling such as "fool" or "Raca," which means "stupid."

Remember the truths of Philippians 2:3-4, and consider your spouse as better than you. Look out for her interests as well as your own. Pray daily for the wisdom to think about James 1:19-20 throughout each day. Be prepared to be a quick listener who is also slow to anger and slow to speak.

Lord, I have to admit that I sometimes blow it in this area. Please give me the self-control to think on my feet. If my wife and I argue, I beseech You to remind me in the heat of the argument that You are not pleased when I stop listening and start hurling angry words.[7]

Practical Tips on Listening and Speaking

BY PHILIP ATTEBERY

- Listen to what is being said rather than planning the next statements you intend to make.

- Eliminate distractions such as loud noises, the telephone, the TV, or computer.

- Repeat what has been said. This helps your wife know you have truly understood what she said and meant.

- Ask questions if you need something clarified.

- Stay on the issue being discussed rather than making it personal. First Corinthians 13:5 declares that love keeps no record of wrongs. That means a loving spouse does not bring up old arguments or issues to use in an attack. Statements such as, "There you go again!" or "You always..." only create hostility and defensiveness.

- Remember that love always hopes for the best (1 Corinthians 13:7). It assumes the best. Assume that your wife is concerned about what is best for you and herself.

- Use "I" centered messages. Make statements such as "I feel discouraged," rather than "You make me so mad!" Center upon your own emotions and feelings, but remain on the real issue. The use of "you" during an argument may cause the listener to be defensive and feel personally attacked.

∞ Remember that love is patient (1 Corinthians 13:4). Wait for the most appropriate time to bring up an important issue. Introducing a big issue when your spouse first comes in the door from a long day at work or after a hectic day of running errands is simply not a good idea.[8]

10

No Strings Attached

BY C.J. SOWELL WITH LYNETTE SOWELL

Husbands ought to love their wives as their own bodies.
He who loves his wife loves himself. After all, no one ever
hated his own body, but he feeds and cares for it.
EPHESIANS 5:28-29

Passage: Ephesians 5:21-33

We guys are pretty competitive creatures. From Little League age on, we learn to keep score. Never let the other dude get more than us. You do me a favor; I do one in return. My buddy's got my back, and I've got his. Traditionally, we learn to give to get. Sometimes even on the job, men figure if they do things for someone else, they can call in a favor in the future.

Marriage isn't—or shouldn't—be like that.

A brother came to me for advice about how to help his wife become more responsive to his initiating lovemaking. He would try to do romantic things for her—flowers, caresses, kisses, or dinner and a movie—with the hope that she'd be more responsive later. Trouble is, the only time he did something special for his wife was when he wanted sex. We guys have needs, which isn't a bad thing. It's how we're wired. And God has given us married guys each an amazing woman with whom we share our lives and can enjoy sharing a bed. But sometimes we forget about her needs. "Husbands, love your wives, just as Christ loved the church and gave himself up for her" (Ephesians 5:25). Our wives are to be cherished and honored. We're not supposed to keep score. We're supposed to sacrifice. Paul goes on in Ephesians 5:28-29 to say, "Husbands ought to love their wives as their own bodies. He who loves his wife loves himself. After all, no one ever hated his own body, but he feeds and cares for it, just as Christ does the church." In other words, Christ is our example. He gives to us because He loves us. In the same way, we shouldn't give to get, but we should give to love.

I suggested to my friend that he do something special for his wife without expecting anything physical in return. Make her favorite meal or order dinner in. Get the kids out of her hair for an evening. Watch a movie she'd like to see. Buy some nice lotion and rub her back or her feet. Or maybe sit on the couch that night or lie in bed and just hold her without trying to initiate anything more. When in a store shopping, he could hold her hand and pretend they're dating. Cherish her and make her feel special—with no strings attached.

Father, give me a new vision of selfless love.[9]

11
Love Always Protects

*[Love] always protects, always trusts,
always hopes, always perseveres.*
1 Corinthians 13:7

Passage: 1 Corinthians 13:1-13

Recently, we had an exciting morning around our house. It all started a few days before when I decided to make scalloped potatoes for dinner. I put too much Velveeta cheese in, and the goo dripped onto the bottom of the stove. That night, I did what I'm famous for. I took the potatoes out, slammed the oven door, and conveniently "forgot" about the swamp of burned cheese on the bottom of my oven.

Daniel and I don't have a self-cleaning oven. Our home is about 45 years old, and I think they bought our oven from Noah before installing it in our home. Anyway, there sat the swamp of burned Velveeta, forgotten…until my kids asked for cheese toast that fine Saturday morning. I was thrilled, of course, since this is a no-brainer breakfast. I flopped several slices of bread on the pan, unwrapped the sliced cheese, dropped the slices on the bread, and popped the whole creation in the oven. I *did* notice the swamp of burned cheese on the bottom of my oven, but I decided that it would probably all cook off in due time. (No one has *ever* accused me of obsessively compulsively cleaning my oven!) Anyway, I meandered down the hallway to check my e-mail.

Soon, I noticed an unusual odor floating from the kitchen. I decided I'd better go check it out. Smoke was roiling from the oven! I looked inside. Let's just say we could have stopped everything right then and had a *wonderful* rendition of "Kumbayah" and a wiener roast with the fire that had erupted in my oven. I grabbed a pot holder, snatched the cheese toast out of the oven, and whacked the oven door closed. A quick inspection of the cheese toast revealed that it was unharmed! Whew! I would have hated having to recook that gourmet breakfast.

Meanwhile, I still had a bonfire blazing in the oven. I stood there and looked through the glass, hoping it would just, well, you know, go out on its own. No luck! Finally, I decided I should try our fire extinguisher. I grabbed the thing, flung open the oven door, and tried to spray. Nothing came out. The fire was still hot and nice and smoky! I slammed the oven door again and peered at the fire extinguisher. I figured now would be a really good time to read the instructions on how to operate that baby. Even after doing everything I was supposed to, I couldn't get anything to come out of the fire extinguisher. Then I remembered the pan of French fries I caught on fire about two years earlier. I'd used the fire extinguisher to put out that blazing inferno. I figured the extinguisher must have gotten clogged up or something.

I still had a bonfire in the oven! I thought about baking soda but couldn't find any. Finally, I decided to do what they told me *not* to do in grade school—throw water on a fire in an electrical appliance. I got a cup of water, opened up the oven door, hurled the liquid inside, and slammed the door before it could do whatever horrendous thing it was going to do that they warned me about in sixth grade. Well, nothing happened, except the fire was now *gone!* Thank the Lord!

When Daniel came home, I told him about everything, and he looked inside the oven. He and I agreed that the time had come to clean out the oven, since it's not a self-cleaner, and I have no memory of cleaning it! I'm sure I must have cleaned it at some point, but I just can't remember it! So he got a spatula and scraped the bottom of the oven. We tackled it with some SOS pads and soon discovered that the bottom of my oven is a lovely shade of gray. How nice!

Before we had kids, my whole house was "furniture store" spotless, and my oven was always clean. Now, cleaning the oven is the last thing on my list. When I'm under a book deadline, *using* the oven is the last thing on my list.

Are you aware of all your wife is doing? If she is working outside the home, has kids, is homeschooling, and expected to keep up with the full-time job of running a household, then she is probably more stressed than you realize.

First Corinthians 13:7 says that love always protects. I believe, as spouses, we each need the other's protection. When I speak to women, I always encourage them to protect their husbands sexually. A man whose wife pours herself into fulfilling his sexual needs will not be weak to the wooing of sexual sin.

Often, men believe that protecting their wives only involves making certain she isn't physically harmed. However, protecting our spouses—whether we're husbands or wives—involves far more than just a one-dimensional approach. One of the many ways you can protect your wife from exhaustion and stress is to help as much as possible with domestic management. Instead of complaining about mishaps and messes, a wise husband pitches in and helps correct the problem.

When Daniel came home and I told him what happened with the oven, he didn't gripe at all. That would have only added to my stress. Instead, we laughed *together,* and then we cleaned the oven *together.*

How do you rank in "domestic stress protection"?

Lord, show me ways I can protect my wife from stress around the house. Please show me how I can be a stress reliever and not a cause of stress.

12

The Helper

*The LORD God said, "It is not good for the man to be alone.
I will make a helper suitable for him."*
GENESIS 2:18

Passage: Genesis 2

"I will make a helper suitable for him." What did God mean? Was He saying that woman was created to only be a helper in the sense of "less than" the man? That a man shouldn't think in terms of helping his wife because being a "helper" is the wife's role?

While no biblical word should ever be isolated to the exclusion of others in order to build unbalanced concepts, consulting word meanings is vitally important to sensible scholarship that breeds integrity in concepts.

Let's look at the word "helper." According to Bible scholar Joseph Coleson,

> English [Bible] versions consistently translate *'ezer* as "helper." This is [a] possible [interpretation], but if we translate it this way, we must avoid the English connotation of someone of inferior status or skill. For example, "carpenter's helper" and "mason's helper" refer to those who do not yet have the skills to be master carpenters or masons. In the Hebrew Scriptures, "helper" means just the opposite. When the Bible speaks of a helper, it usually refers to God the Helper, the Rescuer of those who cannot help themselves. If *'ezer* should be translated "helper" here, it means God intended to make someone who would rescue [Adam] from solitude. This would be God's final step in

making a creature in God's own image, which includes living intimately in community.[10]

Strong's Exhaustive Concordance of the Bible supports this interpretation.[11]

Your wife is much more than your assistant. She is the partner God has given you to honor and cherish with all your being. God will belss you through your wife if you are willing to receive the gift. When you are ill, she will soothe you. When you are discouraged she will uplift you. When you need prayer, she will beseech the Father on your behalf. Just as God Himself is our helper, so your wife can represent His holy presence in your life.

> *Father God, I'm committing anew to begin reading and studying the Bible—and encountering the whole message You have for me. Lord, teach me how to view my wife. Please don't let me live another day without having Your heart and Your eyes in my marriage and in every other aspect of my life.*

13

The True Servant

I am among you as one who serves.
LUKE 22:27

Passage: Luke 22

Recently, Daniel, the kids, and I were staying at a hotel after one of my speaking engagements. Our plane didn't depart until the next morning, so we were enjoying a day of relaxation and family together-time. We decided to order Chinese food for lunch. By the time the man delivered our food, I was so hungry I felt like I could have inhaled the whole meal, Styrofoam containers and all!

We all grabbed plates and started filling them with egg rolls and rice, chicken and broccoli. Between bites, I would pass a requested item to the kids. I was so ravenous, I didn't notice that my husband was the last one to fill his plate. As my stomach began to fill, I saw that he was just beginning. Then I recalled that in the middle of all my chomping, Daniel had carried the weight of serving our children and making certain they had everything they needed. Since we usually share this burden, I felt a tad bit guilty for leaving Daniel to do most of the task alone. But he never complained; instead, he quietly helped our children.

After he had only taken a couple of bites of his meal, Daniel accidentally dropped his plastic fork to the floor. "Oh man," he groaned.

Without another thought, I said, "Here, I'll wash it off for you." I grabbed the fork and began hurrying toward the bathroom.

"You don't have to do that!" Daniel exclaimed.

"No, I insist!" I asserted. "You've been so busy with the kids that you've barely taken a bite yourself while I stuffed my face."

So I scurried into the bathroom, washed off his fork, and returned it with an admiring smile that surged from the appreciation glowing in my heart. Any time I see my husband sacrificing for our children, I fall all over myself to serve him.

Jesus Christ understood selfless love and servanthood. When a person loves and serves selflessly there's no thought for what he will get in return. If my husband had picked up the fork and said, "Here, woman, go wash this off for me," I might have done as he requested...but maybe not. If I had, the task would have generated heavy doses of resentment and zero respect. Instead, I was free to serve my husband with a willing heart, without ever worrying that he would take advantage of my willingness to sacrifice. That is the essence of honest, mutual servanthood.

> *Dear Jesus, give me a new vision of what selfless servanthood is all about. I'm going to sit right here and think on this until You begin to show me ways that I can become more selfless and more like You.*

14

When a Man Loves a Woman

When [he] had received the drink,
Jesus said, "It is finished." With that, he bowed
his head and gave up his spirit.
JOHN 19:30

Passage: John 19

In recent years, Michael Bolton rereleased the classic song "When a Man Loves a Woman." This song details all the things a man in love will do. He can't think of anything else. He'll sleep in the rain for his beloved. He'll even end the relationship with his best friend if the guy insults her. This man puts his woman first in everything. There's nothing in his power that he will deny her.

This secular song puts into words exactly the level of love that wives crave from their husbands. Not only do we want you to feel that love, we want you to *tell* us about it and *show* it to us every day.

Understand that there are differing levels of love. When shallow love approaches the Bible, it looks for a way to elevate the self. This kind of love isolates key scriptures and constructs an argument that makes certain the one loved understands his or her lower status. Or, it adopts attitudes that demean or ridicule the loved person. Men and women both are guilty of such conduct.

If half-grown love reads the Bible, it looks for ways to give of itself...safely. That means certain Bible verses are okay to apply as long as those verses don't stretch half-grown love too much. The "scary" parts of Scripture are the ones that speak of crucifixion and dying to self. Those are usually safely avoided.

When mature love encounters the Word of God, it goes straight to the heart of Christ. This love abandons itself to reading Jesus, studying Jesus, and absorbing the essence of who He was. When a man *really* loves a woman, he'll go through a crucifixion for her. This mature love doesn't center upon the self. Of course, no level of love is required to allow itself to be abused. Nevertheless, mature love's main focus is first upon Christ and then upon the spouse. When both a husband and a wife experience this level of love, they have touched heaven.

> *Dear Jesus, show me what it means to have the level of love You exhibited on the cross. Please don't let me live my whole life and never taste the depth of happiness You can give to my marriage if only I'll let You.*

Take These Hands

BY R.N. HAWKINS

My beloved,

Take these hands I offer this our wedding eve.
Grasp them.

They will feel rough on your slender fingers, don't fear. Yes, they are stained by toil, scarred by labor. These hands I dedicate to you to provide and to protect. In sorrow they will comfort; in achievement they will applaud. You can notice that these hands are strong but as they embrace, caress you, tenderness will be their hallmark.

Across time, in all circumstances, my hands will hold you. They are an extension of my heart, conductors of emotions, expressions of joy and hope. Hand in hand under the grace of God, we will face our tomorrows with faith and fidelity.

With the best of intentions and the strength of my love for you, I realize I'm too weak to maintain what I've promised. So as I offer these hands to you, I ask our Lord and Savior Jesus Christ to cover our hands with His. He alone has the power to hold us together. On Him and His promises we can rely.

Through these hands I give myself to you. They say "I love you."

As you accept them, hold them, I know you are saying, "I love you" back to me.[12]

Notes

Chapter 1—Treat Her Like a Queen

1. Donald M. Joy, and Robbie B. Joy, *Two Become One: God's Blueprint for Couples* (Nappanee, IN: Evangel Publishing House, 2002), pp. 119-23.
2. Adam Clarke, *Adam Clarke's Commentary on the Bible*, abridged by Ralph Earle (Grand Rapids, MI: Baker Book House, 1967), p. 427.
3. R.N. Hawkins, "Romancing." Used by permission.

Chapter 2—Becoming One

1. Jennifer Hale, "What My Husband Does Right." Used by permission.
2. Donald M. Joy, and Robbie B. Joy, *Two Become One: God's Blueprint for Couples* (Nappanee, IN: Evangel Publishing House, 2002), p. 91.
3. Robert M. Hicks, *The Christian Family in Changing Times: The Myths, Models, and Mystery of Family Life* (Grand Rapids, MI: Baker Book House, 2002), p. 65.
4. R.N. Hawkins, "I'd Rather." Used by permission.

Chapter 3—First Bond

1. Paul Hegstrom, *Angry Men and the Women Who Love Them: Breaking the Cycle of Physical and Emotional Abuse* (Kansas City, MO: Beacon Hill Press, 1999), pp. 9-24.
2. Ibid., p. 24.
3. Brian A. Nystrom, MSW, *Ordinary People, Extraordinary Marriages: Reclaiming God's Design for Oneness* (San Jose, CA: Writer's Showcase, 2001), pp. 22-32.
4. Ibid., p. 23.
5. Ibid., p. 25.
6. R.N. Hawkins, "You Color My Life." Used by permission.
7. Hegstrom, *Angry Men*, p. 55.
8. Richard J. Gelles, and Suzanne K. Steinmetz, *Behind Closed Doors: Violence in the American Family* (New York: Anchor Press/Doubleday, 1980), as quoted in Brian A. Nystrom, *Ordinary People*, p. 81.
9. Hegstrom, *Angry Men*, adpated from chart on pp. 30-31, Copyright © Beacon Hill Press of Kansas City. All rights reserved. Used by permission of the publisher.

Chapter 4—Great Sex 101

1. John Temple Bristow, *What the Bible Really Says About Love, Marriage, and Family* (St. Louis: Chalice Press, 1994), pp. 23-33.
2. Walter Wangerin Jr., *As for Me and My House: Crafting Your Marriage to Last* (Nashville: Thomas Nelson, 1990), p. 177.
3. Ibid., p. 178.
4. Willard F. Harley Jr., *His Needs, Her Needs: Building an Affair-Proof Marriage* (Grand Rapids, MI: Fleming H. Revell, 1986), pp. 12-13.
5. Paul Hegstrom, *Angry Men and the Women Who Love Them: Breaking the Cycle of Physical and Emotional Abuse* (Kansas City, MO: Beacon Hill Press, 1999), p. 38.

6. Ibid., 39
7. Robert M. Hicks, *The Christian Family in Changing Times: The Myths, Models, and Mystery of Family Life* (Grand Rapids, MI: Baker Book House, 2002), p. 47.
8. Gary Smalley, with John Trent, *Love Is a Decision: Proven Techniques to Keep Your Marriage Alive and Lively* (Dallas: Word, 1989), p. 51.
9. Douglas Weiss, *Sex, Men, and God: A Godly Man's Road Map to Sexual Success* (Lake Mary, FL: Siloam Press, 2002), p. 118.
10. R.N. Hawkins, "You Honor Me." Used by permission.

Chapter 5—Kids and Chores
1. Stephanie Attebery, "What My Husband Does Right." Used by permission.
2. Robert M. Hicks, *The Christian Family in Changing Times: The Myths, Models, and Mystery of Family Life* (Grand Rapids, MI: Baker Book House, 2002), p. 40.
3. Bryan Chapell, *Each for the Other: Marriage as It's Meant to Be* (Grand Rapids, MI: Baker Book House, 1998), p. 108.
4. R.N. Hawkins, "Her Man." Used by permission.
5. Ronnie Johnson, "Romantic Notions." Used by permission.

Chapter 6—The Truth About Love
1. Jack O. Balswick, and Judith K. Balswick, *The Family: A Christian Perspective on the Contempory Home,* 2nd ed. (Grand Rapids: Baker Book House, 1999), p. 17.
2. Gilbert Bilezikian, *Beyond Sex Roles: A Guide for the Study of Female Roles in the Bible* (Grand Rapids, MI: Baker Book House, 1985), p. 161.
3. Lawrence O. Richards, *The Victor Bible Background Commentary. New Testament* (Colorado Springs: Victor Books, 1994), p. 395.
4. R.N. Hawkins, "It Was Night." Used by permission.
5. Richard Brunstetter, "Romantic Notions." Used by permission.

Chapter 7—Endearing Encounters
1. Lynette Sowell, "What My Husband Does Right." Used by permission.
2. Ronnie Johnson, "Personal Slide Show." Used by permission.
3. Judith Robinson, "Cowboy Firsts." Used by permission.
4. BJ Jensen, "One Hot Mama." Used by permission. (Doug and BJ Jensen are cofounders of Create Loving Relationships Ministries and authors of *Famous Lovers in the Bible and Marriage-Building Secrets We Learn from Them.*)
5. Judith Robinson, "Facing Fears for Each Other." Used by permission.
6. Dean Mills, "Pike's Peak Bubble Bath." Used by permission.
7. Judith Robinson, "Sapphires on a Budget." Used by permission.
8. Ronnie Johnson, "Keeping Romance Alive." Used by permission.
9. Richard L. Brunstetter, "Tropical Paradise." Used by permission.
10. Judith Robinson, "Two to Tango." Used by permission.
11. Richard L. Brunstetter, "Sneaky Fun." Used by permission.
12. Richard L. Brunstetter, "Starry Canopy." Used by permission.
13. Samantha N. Cutshall, "Surprise Date." Used by permission.
14. C.J. Sowell, "Flipping for Flowers." Used by permission.
15. Judith Robinson, "Roses and Coffee." Used by permission.
16. Eric Wiggin, "Rapture Her with Roses." Used by permission.
17. Stan Toler, "The Big Apple." Used by permission.
18. Eric Wiggin, "Money-Saving Travel Tips." Used by permission.

Chapter 8—Rekindling the Flames
1. Alicia Johnson, "What My Husband Does Right." Used by permission.
2. Author unknown, "The Flower," received via e-mail.
3. Chuck Noon, "Looking for Better Opportunities." Used by permission.

4. R.N. Hawkins, prayer. Used by permission.

5. Author unknown, "The Shoe Box," received via e-mail.

6. Ronnie Johnson, "Romance in Crisis." Used by permission.

7. Philip Attebery, "Being Quick to Listen." Used by permission.

8. Philip Attebery, "Practical Tips on Listening and Speaking." Used by permission.

9. C.J. Sowell, with Lynette Sowell, "No Strings Attached." Used by permission.

10. Joseph E. Coleson, *'Ezer Cenegdo: A Power Like Him, Facing Him as Equal*, 3rd ed. (Kansas City, MO: Wesleyan/Holiness Women Clergy, 1996), pp. 11-12.

11. James Strong, LL.D., S.T.D., *The New Strong's Exhaustive Concordance of the Bible* (Nashville: Thomas Nelson Publishers, 1990), "Hebrew and Chaldee Dictionary," 5828 "ezer" and 5826 "azar."

12. R.N. Hawkins, "Take These Hands." Used by permission.

Romancing Your Husband

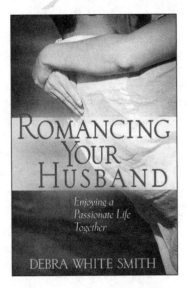

Wives, revolutionize your marriage! This unique book challenges you to cut through traditional misconceptions and explore the total Bible message on marriage. Covers everything from lifting up husbands in prayer to arranging romantic interludes.

See what readers are saying about this book...

"Debra White Smith has hit a home run with *Romancing Your Husband!* The book is replete with great ideas for romance. More importantly, it's from a Christian perspective and tastefully done. The 'Prayer Points' sections provide a marvelous perspective on marriage. I plan to give this book to every couple going through premarital counseling sessions with me."

—Dr. Stan Toler, pastor, author,
and TV host of "Leadership Today"

"Creative, fun, and most of all, vital! *Romancing Your Husband* is a wealth of great ideas that *every* woman should use to put a smile on her husband's face!"

—Bill & Pam Farrel, co-authors of
Men Are Like Waffles—Women Are Like Spaghetti

More Great Books from
Harvest House Publishers

Grace Walk
by Steve McVey

What you've always wanted in the Christian life…but never expected. Learn to push self-sufficiency aside and let Christ live through you. Experience the grace walk and know the spiritual fulfillment you have been yearning for all along.

A Look at Life from a Deer Stand
by Steve Chapman

From the incredible rush of bagging "the big one" to standing in awe of God's magnificent creation, Steve Chapman captures the spirit of the hunt. In short chapters filled with excitement and humor, he takes you to the heart of deer country to discover how the skills necessary for hunting will help you draw closer to the Lord.

Men Are Like Waffles—Women Are Like Spaghetti
by Bill and Pam Farrel

Men keep life elements in separate boxes; women intertwine everything. Providing biblical insights, sound research, and humorous anecdotes, the Farrels explore gender differences and preferences to help you better understand your spouse and strengthen your marriage.

Minute Meditations for Men
by Bob Barnes

Is finding meaningful time with God possible with all the demands on your time? Yes! These two- or three-minute meditations, packed with encouragement, will make an incredible difference in how you handle the day's pressures and maximize your time with God.

Quiet Time for Couples
by H. Norman Wright

Designed to stimulate genuinely open communication between husband and wife, *Quiet Times for Couples* helps you and your spouse develop a closer, more intimate relationship with each other and with God.

Seven Keys to a Healthy Blended Family
by Jim Smoke

Bringing two families together can be daunting. Based on decades of working with divorced and remarried couples, life counselor Jim Smoke offers time-proven principles and wisdom from God's Word to help you deal with new challenges and create a stable, happy family.

Survival Guide for New Dads
by Nick Harrison and Steve Miller

First-time fathers—do not fear! Written by successful dads with grown children, this book provides timely parental insights and devotions based on Scripture and years of experience. Rich with creative and practical advice, *Survival Guide for New Dads* will help you discern priorities, handle the stress of new situations, and pursue excellence in parenting.